Sunset
WOK Cook Book

By the Editors of Sunset Books
and Sunset Magazine

Lane Publishing Co. · Menlo Park, California

Introducing the wok...

Versatility and simplicity are synonymous with wok cooking. With a little practice and our step-by-step directions, you can become adept in no time at using a wok. Here you'll find a host of traditional Oriental recipes—tempura to beef teriyaki—and many Western food surprises—sloppy Joes to corn-on-the-cob.

All of the recipes were tested in the Sunset test kitchens, using a variety of standard woks on electric and gas ranges, as well as electric woks. A special thank you goes to Jan Nix and Fah Liong for their assistance in our many and diverse testing sessions.

SUPERVISING EDITOR
Judith A. Gaulke

SPECIAL CONSULTANT
Linda Anusasananan

DESIGN
Cynthia Hanson

PHOTOGRAPHY
Darrow M. Watt
with Lynne B. Morrall

ILLUSTRATIONS
Mary Davey Burkhardt

COVER
Shrimp-Vegetable Tumble
(page 27)
Photographed by Darrow M. Watt

If your crew is large, you might need one of these oversize woks, but the most practical size for kitchen use is a 14 or 16-inch wok. Our editor visited a wok factory while researching equipment.

Editor, Sunset Books: David E. Clark

Tenth printing April 1986

CONTENTS

SPECIAL FEATURES

WOK COOKERY SIMPLE & FUN

**In all its simplicity, the wok is a
terrifically versatile piece of equipment, a bowl-shaped pan
in which almost any cooking method can be accomplished
and any ingredient cooked.**

Originally, the wok earned its reputation from the stir-fry technique: small pieces of food are toss-cooked in minutes over intense heat. With this technique the colors of vegetables remain bright, the textures crisp, nutrients intact. Meat, poultry, and fish emerge with extraordinary succulence. A stir-fried dish is nutritious, looks fresh, and tastes superb. As a bonus, stir-frying in a wok saves you time and fuel.

If you purchased your wok specifically for Chinese cooking, it may come as a surprise to know that you can use it to prepare Western-style food. In a wok you can scramble eggs, fry tortillas crisp for tacos, make fresh doughnuts, or make a wilted salad. What's more, the wok can double for a deep-fryer and steamer, and it can take the place of a large frying pan in your kitchen. And you can use a wok with equal success on either a gas or electric range.

Choosing a wok…and maintaining it

The traditional bowl-shaped wok is made from heavy-gauge rolled carbon steel, a material that conducts heat well, making this wok especially good for stir-frying and worth a bit of extra effort in seasoning and caring for it. It's true that carbon steel woks will rust if they're not given proper care, but rusting can be avoided.

There are varying theories on how to season a carbon steel wok, but we feel this simple technique is best and easiest. When you first take it home, wash it with sudsy water, then dry it by placing it directly over medium heat on your range for a minute or two. Then rub the inside with about 2 teaspoons of salad oil, taking off the excess oil with a paper towel. After each use, scrub out the wok with a dishwashing brush or bamboo brush and sudsy water, rinse, and dry on the range element again. If the wok is not completely dry when stored, it will rust.

Aluminum and stainless steel woks—often with copper bottoms and sides to improve heat conduction—are also available. They don't rust and are a good choice particularly for steaming and stewing. They're good for stir-frying, too, but heat is not distributed as evenly as with the carbon steel woks. They need no seasoning, and you clean them as you would any other aluminum or stainless steel pan.

The specialty of electric woks is cooking at the table. You can stir-fry, steam, or deep-fry in them. Most of them have a nonstick finish inside. Clean and care for them according to manufacturer's directions, always remembering to remove the heat control before washing.

Woks come in a variety of sizes. For most home cooking, the 14-inch-diameter wok is the most practical, and it's the easiest to store and handle.

Traditional Chinese woks have round bottoms, but some modern woks are now designed with flat bottoms to make them more stable on electric burners.

You'll find variety in handles, too. The traditional wok has two metal handles—one on either side. It is easy to balance on a burner, but you need a potholder to grasp the handle when stir-frying. Some woks now have wooden handle covers. Another wok style has one long wooden handle that can be easily held when stir-frying.

Wok accessories

Special accessories designed for wok cookery are available in cookware shops, but you may find alternatives in your own kitchen that will work just as well. (See equipment photograph on page 7.)

The most useful utensil is a *long-handled spatula* with a wide, curved edge (a regular spatula will do). The dome-shaped *lid* is helpful in stir-frying and is necessary in steaming unless you use Oriental bamboo stacking baskets and lid. A *steaming rack* (metal or bamboo) to place the food above boiling water is also necessary (a round cake rack will do). When steaming or deep-frying, you will find a *ring stand* with slanting sides is helpful for balancing the wok over the range burner

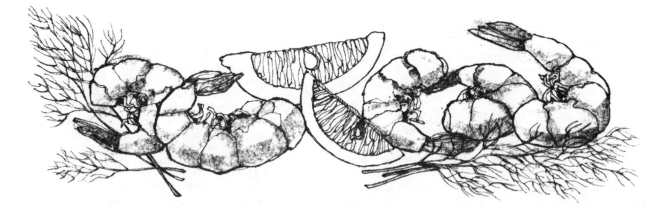

or element. And when you deep-fry in a wok, a little *wire skimmer* is good for removing bits of food from the oil (a large slotted spoon will do). A wire semicircular *draining rack* that attaches to the top of the wok is handy for deep-frying, and a *deep-fat-frying thermometer* will ensure the correct temperatures required in each recipe.

How to use a wok on your range

Woks can be used successfully on either gas or electric ranges. Before you start to cook, experiment with an empty wok to see what arrangement works best on your range for the type of cooking you plan to do. Cooking will vary with each range, but we have prepared our recipes successfully in woks on dozens of different modern electric and gas ranges.

To cook on a gas range, place the wok directly on the metal burner support above the flame. It should rest fairly steadily there. This arrangement should work well for stir-frying. For deep-fat frying or steaming, you may need to stabilize the wok on a ring stand (see photograph on page 7). Place the ring stand on the range, then set the wok on top. Check to see if the wok is within 1 inch of the flame. If not, try turning the ring stand over to bring the wok closer to the burner, or remove the burner support and place the wok stand directly on the cook top.

To cook on an electric range, set the wok directly on the range element for stir-frying. A more stable arrangement is necessary when deep-frying or steaming in a round-bottomed wok. Place the ring stand over the electric element, then suspend the wok in the stand so that it rests directly on the element or within 1-inch of the element (it may be necessary to turn the stand over).

Now you're ready to cook. You'll find our recipes arranged according to cooking method—stir-frying, steaming, and deep-frying. We have focused on these three uses for which the wok is best suited.

The stir-frying technique

The one cooking method that is uniquely Chinese but adaptable to many different foods is stir-frying. It is basic to the recipes in the first half of this book.

Stir-frying is actually quick cooking and stirring of foods in a tiny amount of oil over high heat. Foods aren't really "fried" but are flash-cooked or toss-cooked and seared. Vegetables come out crisp and meats come out tender, with flavor and juices sealed in. To achieve these results, one has to learn to work with higher-than-usual heat. Basically, we take a one-hand-to-cook and one-hand-to-hold-the-wok approach. This allows you to move the wok on and off the heat, if necessary, to control the temperature. The one utensil you'll need is a long-handled spatula. Details on how to stir-fry follow, and recipes begin on page 13.

The cardinal rule is to have everything ready to go before you begin cooking; there's no time to assemble ingredients midstream. You begin by cutting each vegetable and meat called for in a recipe into uniform shapes—usually thin slices or shreds—of a size that will cook tender-crisp in 1 to 2 minutes. (For cutting techniques, see page 9.) Vegetables that require more cooking (such as carrots) may need a little water added to them and a cover placed over them for a few minutes to steam tender. Meat can be marinated ahead, or a little thickening sauce can be added at the last stage of cooking.

The wok should be clean and dry before you start cooking. Place it directly on the element or burner with heat turned to high. Heat the wok hot before adding oil; then always use salad oil

(Continued on page 8)

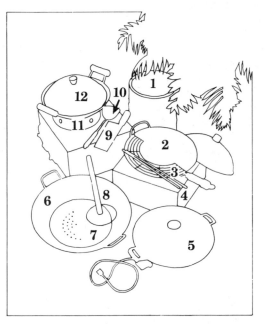

Clockwise: **1.** *Stackable bamboo steamer baskets* **2.** *Flat-bottomed wok with lid and long wooden handle* **3.** *Semicircular attachable wire rack for draining deep-fried foods* **4.** *Bamboo chopsticks* **5.** *Electric wok with lid* **6.** *Metal-handled round-bottomed wok* **7.** *Metal steamer rack* **8.** *Wire skimmer for deep-frying* **9.** *Cleaver* **10.** *Long-handled spatula for stir-frying* **11.** *Metal ring stand for deep-frying and steaming* **12.** *Double-wooden-handled stainless steel wok with copper bottom and lid*

The choices are many when you shop for woks.
Some accessories you might find handy
are shown above and described on page 6.

...The stir-frying technique (cont'd.)

because it can withstand high temperatures without burning. If butter is called for in a recipe, then medium-high heat is best.

When the oil is hot enough to ripple when the wok is tilted from side to side, start cooking.

Add ingredients as the recipe dictates, holding the wok with one hand and stirring and tossing with a long spatula in the other. If the recipe calls for adding ingredients in stages, make sure that each time additional oil is called for, you heat it to rippling hot before adding the next ingredient.

Add a little sauce, if you wish, to thicken and flavor the dish just before serving. Serve immediately.

The deep-frying technique

Crispy deep-fried chicken or fish may be something you never considered doing in a wok. Yet anything that can be done in a deep-fat fryer can be done in a wok, and usually with less oil.

The utensils necessary for deep-frying include a little wire skimmer (or large slotted spoon) for straining off particles of food from the oil before they burn, and a deep-frying thermometer to get correct temperatures required in recipes. Unless you have an electric or flat-bottomed wok, you'll need to use a ring base to give the wok stability when it's filled with hot oil. Place wok on range over high heat and add oil. The high heat is necessary to keep the oil temperature from dropping too low when cold foods are added; for the same reason, add small amounts of food at a time; slide

or lower food into oil carefully to prevent spattering. Handle a wok full of hot oil very carefully with both hands, and allow the oil to cool before you try to pour it out of the wok. You can strain the oil to be used again.

The steaming technique

Steaming foods in a wok is so easy and so satisfactory that you may want to use steaming more often for some of your regular cooking tasks. For example, you can cook a piece of fish or chicken breasts for a salad in steam as fast as in simmering water and with less flavor loss. Flavor accents can be added effectively by sprinkling the food with salt, pepper, or herbs; surrounding it with slices of onion, lemon, or ginger; or drizzling soy over it.

A lid and a metal rack—one made especially for the wok, or just a round cake rack—are all you need to convert your wok to a steamer. Also available are handsome bamboo baskets that stack, so several things can steam on different layers at once.

Set the food directly on the rack so there is room for the steam to circulate, and keep an inch or more of water simmering under the rack. Put the lid on the wok and allow about the same cooking time as for foods simmering in water.

Oriental bamboo stacking baskets for steaming (see photograph on page 7) make it possible to steam several foods at once. You buy each basket separately. Also available separately is a lid for the baskets. This bamboo lid means you don't have to own a wok lid in order to use your wok for steaming. But its main advantage is that it is designed to minimize condensation. If you use the metal wok lid, drops of water will form on it, and you may want to lay a piece of wax paper or foil over certain foods (custards, for instance) during steaming.

Braising and stewing technique

This cooking method—browning meat in a little oil before adding it to a dish to be cooked in liquid—is best done in a wok other than carbon steel. The wok shape is fine for stews and soups, but we found lengthy cooking in liquid in carbon steel woks often produced a metallic taste in the foods.

You braise the meat in oil as in stir-frying, then stir-fry vegetables, add liquid, and simmer, covered, until tender. Remember when cooking with large amounts of liquid, set the conventional wok on a ring stand to stabilize it.

The art of slicing and chopping

For stir-frying, it is important to have all ingredients cut the same size and shape for even, quick cooking. Oriental cooks take great pride in food presentation and eye appeal. Vegetables are made even more beautiful with uniform slicing and chopping. Meats cut thin are tender and succulent when stir-fried.

Cutting in slanting or diagonal slices is a very effective way to cut through fibrous vegetables (such as celery) and meats (such as flank steak) to tenderize them and expose the largest area to the heated wok sides during cooking.

To slice meat, start with it partially frozen for easier handling. With a very sharp knife or cleaver, cut across the grain of the meat at a 45° angle. Our recipes usually call for cutting meat and vegetables into ¼ to ⅛-inch-thick slanting slices (see illustrations below).

If a recipe calls for foods to be sliced thin, it usually means cutting straight down, not at a slant (see illustration below). Cutting in matchstick-size pieces refers to cutting vegetables or poultry in thin strips about the length and width of a wooden match. Dicing means cutting in small squares.

Some special ingredients

For the recipes in this book, we've tried to concentrate on ingredients you already know. A few, though, might be less familiar. The photograph on page 10 will help you identify them more quickly, and you may want to take this book along to the market on your next trip. Most of these foods can be found in the produce or Oriental section of your market. Some, such as water chestnuts and bean sprouts, may only be available canned. Others, such as edible-pod peas, may come only in frozen packages.

Baby corn. Miniature corn cobs are really a special variety of corn-on-the cob. (See photograph on page 10.) They are available canned in water or pickled, but our recipes call only for those packed in water. They are sweet and tender—you eat the cob and all.

Bamboo shoots. Available canned, they come whole or sliced. Light yellow in color, they are tender and fibrous with a little sweetness that comes alive when cooked.

Bean sprouts. Two to 3-inch-long sprouted mung beans are available canned and fresh, either packaged or loose. Translucent and crisp, they add crunch to any dish. (See photograph on page 10.)

Bean threads. Before they are cooked, these Oriental noodles look like stiff nylon fishing line, but they puff up crisp when dropped into hot oil. Sometimes they are called Chinese vermicelli or translucent noodles.

Bok choy (Chinese white cabbage). A tender-crisp, sweet, very mild vegetable consisting of a clump of snow-white stalks ending in wide, dark green leaves. (See photograph on page 10.)

Cashew nuts. Familiar to most as a snack to nibble, they appear in our recipes whole or chopped as a flavorful garnish for a variety of dishes. (See photograph on page 10.)

Chinese cabbage (napa or celery cabbage). Mild, delicate, crisp-textured—these words describe the solid, oblong head of wide, celerylike stalks ending in frilly, pale green leaves. (See photograph on page 10.)

Chinese five-spice. This Oriental blend of ground cloves, fennel, licorice root, cinnamon, and star anise is bottled by American spice companies and readily available. As a substitute, try mixing ½

(Continued on page 11)

Cutting in slanting or diagonal slices or into uniform pieces of equal thickness is a very effective way to cut through fibrous vegetables and meats to tenderize them and expose the largest area to the heated wok sides during cooking.

*Colorful ingredients make beautiful dishes. Use this photograph
as a grocery guide for those that are unfamiliar;
all are identified on page 11.*

teaspoon ground ginger, ¼ teaspoon *each* ground cinnamon and crushed anise seed, and ⅛ teaspoon *each* ground allspice and cloves.

Chinese noodles (mein). Noodles of wheat flour, with or without egg, may be labeled nothing more than "mein" or the word may not be on the package at all. They come dried or fresh in packages of looped or curly bundles.

Coriander (cilantro and Chinese parsley). Grown from the whole coriander spice seed, this green broadleaf parsley is a pungent and powerful flavor addition. It doesn't taste a thing like regular parsley. (See photograph on page 10.)

Dried mushrooms. These come in several sizes in cellophane packages weighing about an ounce. They have to be reconstituted in warm water for about half an hour. Always cut away the stems after soaking, and squeeze out the soaking liquid from the mushrooms before slicing or dicing. They have a firm, rubbery texture and woodsy perfume. (See photograph on page 10.)

Edible-pod peas (snow peas, sugar peas, or Chinese pea pods). Available fresh or frozen, they are crisp, flat, bright green, tender pods with tiny, underdeveloped peas inside. The fresh ones need to have ends and strings removed before they're cooked. Snap off the stem end and pull the strings straight down the pod sides. (See photograph on page 10.)

Eggplant. Plump, purple, and pear-shaped, eggplant has shiny skin and a firm, pulpy interior. Small varieties are called Oriental eggplant and can be used interchangeably with the larger types. (See photograph on page 10.)

Fermented black beans. Used for sauces, they are available dried and whole in plastic bags in your market. They have a very pungent flavor for their size. (See photograph on page 10.)

Garlic. Of the onion family, garlic cloves, when peeled and minced or pressed, exude a very strong, hot aroma. (See photograph on page 10.)

Ginger root. The fresh, light brown root is very hot and nippy. A little goes a long way. You can freeze it for long storage and use it without thawing. Peel it, then grate, slice, or chop to use. When substituting ground ginger, use only about one-half as much. (See photograph on page 10.)

Leeks. Resembling large green onions, leeks are milder in flavor and more fibrous than their cousins. (See photograph on page 10.)

Oyster sauce. This bottled brown sauce has a rich subtle flavor stemming from oysters. It is used in many Oriental-style dishes.

Rice noodles. These dried, opaque, white, thin noodles made of rice are also called mai fun or rice sticks. (See photograph on page 10.)

Sausage. Chinese sausage are red and white in color and mildly sweet and spicy in flavor. They can be steamed with rice or other ingredients or stir-fried. (See photograph on page 10.)

Sesame seed. When toasted, sesame seed takes on a sweet and nutlike flavor and is often used as garnish for our recipes. Sesame oil is a by-product.

Soy sauce. The dark, savory, salty sauce is made from soybeans and wheat flour. It is one of the most-used and most versatile sauces in Oriental cuisines, and it varies in strength from brand to brand.

Tofu (soybean curd). A high-protein product made from cooked soybeans, tofu comes in several forms—soft to firm—as well as in deep-fried puffs. See the special feature on tofu, page 38.

Water chestnuts. Peeled, packed in water, and canned, the water chestnut is crisp and crunchy with a sweet flavor. Fresh water chestnuts are available at certain times of the year in Oriental markets. To prepare them, pare off the thin, dark brown, scaly skin and use "meat" as if canned. To store canned or fresh chestnuts, cover with water and refrigerate; change water every other day.

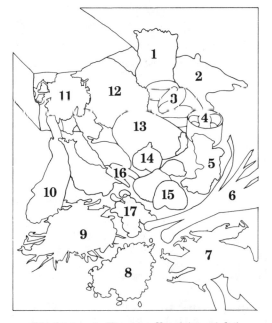

Clockwise: **1.** *Rice noodles (rice sticks)*
2. *Roast duck* **3.** *Chinese sausage* **4.** *Canned water chestnuts* **5.** *Fresh ginger root*
6. *Leeks* **7.** *Edible-pod peas (pea pods, sugar peas, or snow peas)* **8.** *Fermented black beans* **9.** *Bean sprouts* **10.** *Bok choy*
11. *Coriander (cilantro or Chinese parsley)* **12.** *Chinese cabbage (napa or celery cabbage)* **13.** *Eggplant* **14.** *Garlic clove* **15.** *Dried mushrooms* **16.** *Baby corn*
17. *Cashew nuts*

STIR-FRYING IN A WOK

If you've ever watched a Chinese chef cook in a wok,
you must have been amazed at how quickly and deftly he worked, turning
out wonderfully crisp vegetables and tender meats in a matter
of minutes. The secret is in the technique known as stir-frying.
Small pieces of food are cooked in a small amount of oil
in a very hot wok; the food is tossed—stir-fried—
constantly so that it is quickly seared on all sides to maintain the
vegetables' crisp texture and the meat's flavorful juices.

How to stir-fry in a wok

Stir-frying works well with almost any kind of meat, poultry, and seafood, and with a variety of vegetables. In this chapter we give you recipes for a myriad of different combinations and seasonings. And once you master the basics, you can create your own recipes with foods on hand.

Though our recipes give average cooking times, we suggest you take them with a grain of salt. They are only a guide, and actual cooking times will vary with the kind of wok you use and the intensity of your heat source.

Here are the seven steps to stir-frying:

1. Do all your cutting in advance. Foods should be cut in small, uniform pieces (usually thin slices or pieces) that will cook in a few minutes. (See page 9 for cutting instructions.) Keep each ingredient separate.

2. Prepare any seasonings and sauce mixtures in advance. Once you start cooking, you won't be able to stop to mix a sauce.

3. Assemble the cut meat and/or vegetables, seasonings, sauce mixture, and salad oil nearby.

4. Place the wok (it should be clean and dry) over high heat. When the wok is hot, add salad oil (about 2 tablespoons per pound of cut-up vegetables or meat). Heat the oil until it is hot enough to ripple when the wok is tilted from side to side.

5. Holding the wok handle with one hand, add any seasoning (such as garlic or ginger). With a wide spatula in your other hand, stir and toss until the seasoning is lightly browned. Add meat, if used, all at once—never add more than about ½ pound at a time; if you have more, cook it in several batches, adding oil as needed. Stir and toss the meat so that all pieces come in contact with the hot wok surface until lightly browned. Turn out of wok.

6. Add 1 to 2 tablespoons more oil. When the oil is hot, add the vegetables, cooking one variety at a time, starting with those that take the longest to cook (see the vegetable chart on page 14 for cooking times). With the wide spatula, stir-fry the vegetables, coating them with oil. If a vegetable is very dense or fibrous (such as broccoli or asparagus), you may need to add a few tablespoons water, then cover and steam the vegetables slightly, stirring frequently. Remove the cooked vegetables. Add any remaining vegetables in sequence according to their cooking time, stir-frying after each addition until all vegetables are tender-crisp.

7. Return the cooked meat and vegetables to the wok and add cooking sauce or cornstarch mixture to flavor or thicken the dish. Cook, stirring, until the liquid boils and thickens. Serve.

Sesame Cauliflower Stir-fry

Generous amounts of parsley and green onion give color and freshness to this quickly cooked vegetable dish. Squeeze lemon juice over individual servings.

    ¼ cup sesame seed
    4 tablespoons butter or margarine
    1 small onion, finely chopped
    1 head cauliflower (about 1½ lbs.),
         broken into flowerets, then cut in
         ⅛-inch slices
    ¼ cup water
    ½ cup thinly sliced green onion
    ¼ cup chopped parsley
       Salt and pepper
       Lemon wedges

Place wok over medium heat. When wok is hot, add sesame seed and stir occasionally until golden (about 1 minute); remove from wok and set aside.

Add butter to wok. When butter has melted, turn heat to medium-high, add onion, and stir-fry until limp (about 1 minute). Add cauliflower and stir-fry for about 30 seconds. Add water; cover and cook, stirring frequently, for about 2 minutes or until tender-crisp. Stir in green onion, parsley, sesame seed, and salt and pepper to taste; stir-fry for about 1 minute. Serve with lemon wedges to squeeze over. Makes 6 to 8 servings.

Italian-style Vegetables

Lots of garlic permeates these vegetables, making the dish a favorite among lovers of Italian food.

    2 tablespoons salad oil
    3 to 4 cloves garlic, minced or pressed
    1 onion, finely chopped
    2 large zucchini, cut in ¼-inch slices
    1 package (9 oz.) frozen Italian green
         beans, thawed
    1 can (14 oz.) Italian-style tomatoes,
         drained and chopped
    1 teaspoon Italian seasoning or ¼
         teaspoon *each* dry basil, thyme,
         oregano, and marjoram leaves
    1 can (2¼ oz.) sliced ripe olives, drained

Place wok over high heat. When wok is hot, add oil. When oil is hot, add garlic, onion, and zucchini; stir-fry for about 2 minutes. Add green beans and stir-fry for about 2 minutes. Add tomatoes, Italian seasoning, and olives; stir-fry for about 1 minute or until heated through. Makes 4 to 6 servings.

Stir-frying vegetables

When combining several vegetables for an all-vegetable stir-fry dish, keep this in mind: because of texture differences, each vegetable has its own cooking time. For example, thin slices of carrot are dense and will take longer to cook than thin slices of celery, which are watery. With dense vegetables, it is necessary to add a small amount of water to the wok part way through cooking, and then cover the wok; this process steams the vegetables to the tender-crisp state.

If you cook a dish that calls for several vegetables and the textures are different, add the firmest vegetable to the wok and cook for the time indicated below; then add the more tender vegetables near the end of the cooking time. Or better yet, you can cook each vegetable separately and combine them for reheating and blending of flavors.

To stir-fry vegetables, place the wok over high heat. When the wok is hot, add 1 tablespoon oil for 1 pound of vegetables. (Remember, don't fill the wok too full, for the whole point of stir-frying is to expose the maximum food surface to the heated wok sides.) When the oil is hot, add the vegetables all at once and stir-fry for 1 minute; then add the amount of liquid and either continue stir-frying or cover and cook for the remaining time indicated in the chart. If covered, lift the lid and stir once or twice during cooking, adding a few drops of water if pan appears dry. The vegetables listed below are the best ones to stir-fry.

Each pound of vegetables makes 2 or 3 servings.

Vegetable (1 lb.)	Tablespoons salad oil	Minutes to stir-fry	Tablespoons broth or water	Minutes to cover & cook
Asparagus (Cut in ½-inch slanting slices)	1	1	1	3
Beans, green (Cut in 1-inch pieces)	1	1	5	4
Bok choy (Leaves cut in 1-inch strips, stalks cut in ¼-inch strips)	1	3	1	—
Broccoli (Cut in small flowerets, then in ½-inch pieces)	1	1	3	3
Brussels sprouts (Cut in half)	1	1	4	5
Cabbage (Cut in ¼-inch shreds)	1	1	—	2
Carrots (Cut in ¼-inch slices)	1	1	2	3
Cauliflower (Cut in small flowerets, then in ½-inch pieces)	1	1	3	4
Celery (Cut in ¼-inch slices)	1	3	1	—
Edible-pod peas (Stems and strings removed)	1	3	1	—
Mushrooms (Cut in ¼-inch slices)	1	3	1	—
Pepper, green bell (Cut in 1-inch chunks)	1	1	2	2
Swiss chard (Cut in 1-inch slices)	1	4	—	—
Zucchini and summer squash (Cut in ¼-inch slices)	1	1	1	3

*Two in the kitchen make stir-frying easier: one to
prepare ingredients, the other to cook.
The recipe for egg foo yung (foreground) is on page 22.*

Sweet and Sour Soybeans

Soybeans have come into their own popularity. High in protein, they take the place of meat in this sweet and sour dish. You have to plan ahead to soak and simmer the beans before you stir-fry.

> 1 cup dried soybeans
> Water
> Sweet and sour sauce (directions follow)
> 2 tablespoons salad oil
> 1 large onion, cut in 1-inch chunks
> 2 large carrots, cut in ¼-inch slices
> 1 clove garlic, minced or pressed
> 2 tablespoons water
> 1 green pepper, seeded and cut in 1-inch squares
> ¾ cup fresh pineapple chunks or canned pineapple chunks, drained
> 2 small tomatoes, cut in 1-inch chunks

Rinse soybeans, place in a 3-quart pan, and cover with 3 cups water. Cover and soak for at least 6 hours or overnight. Drain beans, pouring liquid through a wire strainer into a bowl; discard loose fibrous bean skins.

Combine beans and soaking liquid again in pan, adding more water if necessary to cover beans. Cover and simmer for 3 hours or until beans are tender to bite; while cooking, stir several times and add more water if needed to prevent sticking. Drain, reserving ¼ cup liquid for sweet and sour sauce; discard loose bean skins.

Prepare sweet and sour sauce and set aside.

Place wok over high heat. When wok is hot, add oil. When oil is hot, add onion, carrots, and garlic; stir-fry for 1 minute. Add water; cover and cook for 2 minutes, stirring frequently, until vegetables are tender-crisp. Add green pepper; stir-fry for about 1 minute. Add pineapple, tomatoes, soybeans, and sweet and sour sauce. Stir until mixture boils and thickens and vegetables are coated with sauce (about 2 minutes). Serves 4.

Sweet and sour sauce. Stir together 1 tablespoon **cornstarch**, ⅓ cup firmly packed **brown sugar**, ¼ teaspoon **ground ginger**, 1 tablespoon *each* **soy sauce** and **dry sherry**, 5 tablespoons **wine vinegar**, and ¼ cup reserved **cooking liquid** or regular-strength beef broth.

Mediterranean Vegetables

Here's a colorful vegetable combination that stars eggplant—making a dish reminiscent of ratatouille. Parmesan cheese melts on top.

> 3 tablespoons olive oil or salad oil
> 1 large onion, cut in ½-inch slices
> 1 medium-size eggplant, unpeeled, cut in ½-inch cubes
> 3 to 4 tablespoons water
> ½ teaspoon *each* basil and oregano leaves
> ⅛ teaspoon pepper
> 1 cup sliced celery
> 1 medium-size green pepper, seeded and cut in 1-inch squares
> 1 medium-size tomato, peeled and cut in wedges
> ½ cup grated Parmesan cheese

Place wok over medium heat. When wok is hot, add oil. When oil is hot, add onion and eggplant; stir-fry for about 30 seconds or until vegetables are coated with oil. Add water; cover and cook for about 8 minutes, stirring often. Stir in basil, oregano, pepper, celery, and green pepper; cover and cook, stirring often, for about 5 minutes longer or until vegetables are tender-crisp.

Arrange tomato wedges on top, cover wok, and cook for about 1 minute. Sprinkle cheese over; cover wok for about 1 minute to melt cheese; then serve. Makes 4 to 6 servings.

Wilted salads in a wok

To whet your appetite, many restaurants prepare hot salads right before your eyes. You can make these dramatic presentations for your guests too. Just use an electric wok at the table.

Of course, you can always make your salad in the kitchen in a regular wok and then transfer it to individual salad plates or a large salad bowl to serve. Try an assortment of greens for variety.

Wilted Romaine Salad

- 1 small head (¾ lb.) romaine lettuce
- 2 tablespoons lemon juice
- 1 tablespoon *each* sugar and catsup
- ½ teaspoon *each* Worcestershire and Dijon mustard
- ¼ cup salad oil
- 1 medium-size onion, chopped
- ¼ pound bean sprouts
- 1 cup seasoned croutons

Tear romaine in bite-size pieces and set aside. Mix lemon juice, sugar, catsup, Worcestershire, and mustard and set aside.

Turn electric wok to high heat or set regular wok over high heat. When wok is hot, add oil. When oil is hot, add onion and stir-fry for about 1 minute or until onion is limp. Add lemon juice mixture. When mixture boils, add romaine. Turn off heat or remove wok from range. Add sprouts and croutons and toss until lettuce is coated with dressing. Makes 4 servings.

Hot Spinach Salad

- Mustard dressing (directions follow)
- 2 bunches (¾ to 1 lb. *each*) spinach
- 4 strips bacon, cut in 1-inch pieces
- 1 hard-cooked egg, finely chopped
- Lemon wedges

Prepare mustard dressing and set aside.

Remove tough stems from spinach. Break leaves into bite-size pieces and set aside.

Turn electric wok to medium heat or set regular wok over medium heat. When wok is hot, add bacon pieces. Stir-fry until crisp (about 2 minutes). Discard all but 1 tablespoon drippings. Stir in spinach and toss just until all leaves are coated and begin to wilt (about 1 minute). Turn off heat or remove wok from range, drizzle mustard dressing over, and toss until blended. Serve on individual plates, sprinkle with chopped egg, and offer lemon wedges to squeeze over. Makes 4 servings.

Mustard dressing. In a blender combine ⅓ cup **salad oil**, 2 tablespoons **tarragon wine vinegar**, 1 tablespoon **Dijon mustard**, 1 teaspoon *each* **shallots** and **sugar**, and ¼ teaspoon **salt**. Whirl until smooth.

Hot Iceberg Salami Salad

- 3 tablespoons wine vinegar
- 2 teaspoons sugar
- 1 teaspoon dry basil
- ¼ teaspoon salt
- ⅛ teaspoon pepper
- ¼ pound sliced dry salami, cut in ¼-inch strips
- Olive oil or salad oil
- 1 small red onion, thinly sliced
- 1 clove garlic, minced or pressed
- 1 small head (about 1 lb.) iceberg lettuce, torn into bite-size pieces
- ¼ pound chicory, torn into bite-size pieces
- 1 jar (4 oz.) diced pimentos, drained
- Salt and pepper

Mix together vinegar, sugar, basil, salt, and pepper and set aside.

Turn electric wok to medium heat or set regular wok over medium heat. When wok is hot, add salami and stir-fry until lightly browned (about 1 minute); remove salami from wok and set aside. Add enough oil to drippings to make a total of ¼ cup oil. Add onion and garlic; stir-fry for about 30 seconds. Add vinegar mixture and heat until it boils; turn off heat or remove wok from range. Stir in lettuce, chicory, and pimento just to heat through. Season with salt and pepper to taste. Makes 4 to 6 servings.

*Italian carbonara in a wok makes
a showy presentation when brought to the table for serving.
The recipe is on page 20.*

Edible-pod Peas with Celery

Snow peas, often called edible-pod peas (see photograph on page 10), are easy to trim—just snap off the stem end, then pull the strings down the pod sides. They add crunch and color to any dish.

   1 tablespoon cornstarch
   ½ teaspoon salt
   1 teaspoon sugar
   1 tablespoon soy sauce
   ½ cup water
   2 tablespoons salad oil
   ½ cup sliced green onion
   4 stalks celery, cut in ¼-inch slanting slices
   1 pound edible-pod peas or 2 packages (6 oz. *each*) frozen edible-pod peas, thawed
   1 tablespoon water

Stir together cornstarch, salt, sugar, soy, and the ½ cup water; set aside.

Place wok over high heat. When wok is hot, add oil. When oil is hot, add onion, celery, and peas; stir-fry for about 3 minutes (1 minute if frozen) or until onion is limp; add the 1 tablespoon water, if needed. Add cornstarch mixture and stir-fry until it boils and thickens (about 2 minutes). Makes 4 to 6 servings.

Forest Mushrooms and Cabbage

Oriental mushrooms, also called forest mushrooms, are most commonly available in dried form (see photograph on page 10); look for them in Oriental markets. To restore their rich, distinctive flavor, you must first soak them for a while in warm water.

   ¾ ounce Oriental dried mushrooms (about 3 large mushrooms)
     Warm water
   1 small head (about 1¼ lbs.) cabbage
   2 tablespoons salad oil
   1 clove garlic, minced or pressed
   1 tablespoon soy sauce
     Salt and pepper
     Chopped parsley or sliced green onion (optional)

Cover mushrooms with warm water and soak until soft (about 20 minutes). Trim off and discard hard stem portion; rinse mushrooms well, pat dry, and slice into ½-inch-wide strips; set aside.

Cut cabbage into 1 by 2-inch pieces.

Place wok over high heat. When wok is hot, add oil. When oil is hot, add garlic and mushrooms; stir-fry for about 1 minute. Add cabbage and soy; stir-fry for about 1 minute, cover and cook 2 minutes, stirring frequently, until cabbage is tender-crisp. Season to taste with salt and pepper. Sprinkle with parsley, if desired. Makes 4 servings.

Broccoli with Fresh Mushrooms

Bright green broccoli makes an attractive dish to accompany fish or poultry. Broccoli lovers may even want to make a meal of this dish.

   2 tablespoons salad oil
   1 pound broccoli, cut in small flowerets, with thick stems cut in ⅛-inch slices
   1 teaspoon sugar
   ½ teaspoon salt
   1 tablespoon water
   ½ pound mushrooms, cut in ¼-inch slices
   2 green onions, finely chopped
   ¼ teaspoon ground nutmeg
     Dry-roasted cashews or filberts (optional), chopped

Place wok over high heat. When wok is hot, add 1 tablespoon of the oil. When oil is hot, add broccoli, sugar, and salt; stir-fry for 1 minute. Add water,

(Continued on next page)

cover and cook, stirring frequently, until broccoli is tender-crisp (about 3 minutes), adding more water, if needed; remove from wok and set aside.

Add remaining 1 tablespoon oil. When oil is hot, add mushrooms, onions, and nutmeg; stir-fry until liquid evaporates (about 3 minutes). Return broccoli to wok and stir to heat through. Top with nuts, if you like. Makes 4 to 5 servings.

Garden Scramble Stir-fry

Brilliant green broccoli combines with garden-fresh carrots and cauliflower for this vegetable main dish. Garnish with whole cashews.

> 2 tablespoons salad oil
> 1 large clove garlic, minced or pressed
> 1 cup broccoli flowerets, cut in
>   ½-inch chunks
> 1 cup cauliflower flowerets, cut in
>   ½-inch chunks
> 3 tablespoons water
> ½ cup carrots, cut in ½-inch
>   slanting slices
> ½ red bell pepper, cut in ¼-inch strips
>   Salt and pepper
>   Whole cashews

Place wok over high heat. When wok is hot, add 1 tablespoon of the oil. When oil is hot, add garlic and stir-fry for 30 seconds. Add broccoli and cauliflower and stir-fry for 1 minute. Add 2 tablespoons of the water; cover and cook, stirring frequently, for about 3 minutes. Remove from wok and set aside.

Add remaining 1 tablespoon oil to wok. When oil is hot, add carrots and red pepper. Stir-fry for 1 minute. Add remaining 1 tablespoon water; cover and cook, stirring frequently, for about 2 minutes or until vegetables are tender-crisp. Return broccoli and cauliflower to wok and stir-fry to heat through (about 1 minute). Add salt and pepper to taste and garnish with cashews. Makes 2 or 3 servings.

Chard and Cabbage Stir-fry

When you start out with two whole heads of greens, you may think they'll never fit into your wok. Surprisingly, they wilt down to less than half the volume you started with.

> 1 small head (about 1¼ lbs.) cabbage
> 1 bunch (about 1¼ lbs.) Swiss chard
> 2 tablespoons sesame seed
> 3 strips bacon, cut in ½-inch pieces
> 1 large onion, thinly sliced
> 1 clove garlic, minced or pressed
> 1 tablespoon *each* soy sauce and water

Finely shred cabbage (you should have about 5 cups). Cut white center stalks from leafy green part of chard; thinly slice stalks, then slice leafy parts, keeping separate.

Place wok over medium heat. When wok is hot, add sesame seed and stir-fry until golden (about 30 seconds). Remove seed from wok and set aside. Turn heat to medium-high; add bacon and stir-fry until crisp (about 2 minutes). Remove bacon from wok; drain and set aside. Leave 1 tablespoon bacon drippings in wok; set remaining drippings aside.

Turn heat to high. Add onion and stir-fry for about 2 minutes. Add cabbage and chard stalks; stir-fry for about 4 minutes, adding more bacon drippings if needed. Combine garlic, soy, and water; add to wok along with chard leaves and stir-fry for about 2 minutes or until wilted. Sprinkle with bacon and sesame seed. Makes 6 servings.

Carbonara

Pictured on page 18

Beaten egg is the secret of this delicate and delicious sauce; it coats the tagliarini or spaghetti and causes the bits of cheese and meat to cling evenly. Carbonara makes a dramatic entrée when assembled at the table. Or serve it as a first course, if you like—then it serves 6 to 8.

> ¼ pound mild Italian pork sausage
> ½ pound prosciutto (finely chopped) or
>   cooked ham (thinly sliced)
> 2 tablespoons butter or margarine
> ½ cup lightly packed minced parsley
> 3 eggs, beaten
> ½ cup freshly grated or shredded
>   Parmesan cheese
>   Pepper
>   About ½ pound hot cooked and
>   drained tagliarini or spaghetti
>   Additional grated or shredded
>   Parmesan cheese

Remove casings from sausage; crumble sausage.

Place wok over medium heat. When wok is hot, add sausage and half the prosciutto; stir-fry for about 5 minutes or until lightly browned. Blend remaining half of prosciutto with cooked sausage mixture; remove wok from heat.

(If you like, the following steps can be completed at the table. Have ready, in separate containers, butter, parsley, eggs, and the ½ cup cheese, as well as a pepper mill.)

Add hot tagliarini, butter, and parsley to meats. Mix quickly to blend. At once pour in eggs and continue to blend, quickly lifting and mixing the pasta to coat well with egg. Sprinkle in the ½ cup cheese and a dash of pepper; mix again. Serve with additional cheese. Makes 4 servings.

Fettucini Verde

A cream coating glistens on the light green vegetable noodles used in this version of a first-course Italian classic. For a dramatic presentation, cook it at the table in an electric wok.

    6 tablespoons butter or margarine,
        cut in chunks
    1 cup chopped green onion
        (including some of the tops)
    2 cloves garlic, minced or pressed
    3 to 4 cups hot cooked and drained
        vegetable noodles
    1 cup whipping cream
      About 1 cup grated Parmesan cheese
      Salt and pepper
      Ground nutmeg
      Additional grated Parmesan cheese

Place wok over medium-high heat. When wok is hot, add butter. When butter has melted, add onion and garlic. Stir-fry until onion is limp (about 2 minutes).

Add cooked noodles and cream. Stir to mix over high heat until cream just begins to boil. Sprinkle with cheese, then toss and mix until noodles are well coated. Season with salt, pepper, and nutmeg to taste. Pass additional Parmesan cheese to sprinkle over, if desired. Makes 4 servings.

Fried Rice with Peas

Hot pepper seasoning and lemon peel are the tart surprise in this fried rice dish. For a green and white accompaniment to butter-sautéed fish, choose this.

    4 tablespoons butter or margarine
    ½ cup sliced green onion
    ¼ cup minced parsley
    1 package (10 oz.) frozen peas, thawed
    4 cups cold cooked rice
    2 teaspoons grated lemon peel
    2 tablespoons soy sauce
      Dash liquid hot pepper seasoning

Place wok over medium-high heat. When wok is hot, add butter. When butter has melted, add onion and parsley. Stir-fry until onion is limp (about 1 minute). Turn heat to high and add peas, rice, lemon peel, soy, and hot pepper seasoning. Stir-fry until heated through, adding more butter if needed. Makes 4 servings.

Fried Brown Rice with Vegetables

For a different twist, try brown rice instead of white. A sprinkling of chopped fresh coriander just before serving gives added flavor.

      About 3 tablespoons salad oil
    1 cup thinly sliced carrots
    1 medium-size onion, thinly sliced
    1 clove garlic, minced or pressed
    1 large green pepper, seeded and cut
        in thin strips
    1 cup thinly sliced zucchini
    1 cup thinly sliced mushrooms
    1 tablespoon water (optional)
    2 cups bean sprouts
    1 cup cold cooked brown rice
    4 tablespoons soy sauce
      Chopped fresh coriander (cilantro)

Place wok over high heat. When wok is hot, add 1 tablespoon of the oil. When oil is hot, add carrots and stir-fry for about 1 minute. Add onion, garlic, and green pepper. Stir-fry for about 1 minute, adding more oil as needed. Add zucchini and mushrooms. Stir-fry for about 2 minutes or until all vegetables are just tender-crisp, adding water, if needed. Add bean sprouts and rice, stirring to heat through. Stir in soy. Sprinkle with coriander. Makes 6 to 8 servings.

Egg Foo Yung

Pictured on page 15

You can enjoy a completely meatless entrée with these little egg patties, or make them with crab, shrimp, or poultry. It's easier to fry two at a time, but three will fit in a flat-bottomed wok.

Foo yung sauce (directions follow)
4 eggs, beaten
½ pound bean sprouts
⅓ cup thinly sliced green onions
½ pound cooked crab, small cooked shrimp, or slivered cooked chicken (optional)
⅛ teaspoon *each* garlic powder and pepper
½ teaspoon salt
About 2 tablespoons salad oil

Prepare foo yung sauce and keep warm. Combine eggs, bean sprouts, onion, crab (if desired), garlic powder, pepper, and salt (omit salt if using canned crab).

Place wok over medium-high heat. When wok is hot, add oil. When oil is hot, add ¼ cup of the egg mixture for each patty (make 2 or 3 at a time). Fry, turning once when lightly browned and cooked to your liking (about 2 minutes on each side). Continue with remaining batter until all patties are cooked, adding more oil as needed. Remove to warm platter and pour foo yung sauce over patties. Makes 6 servings.

Foo yung sauce. Place wok over low heat. When wok is hot, add 1 teaspoon **cornstarch**, 1 teaspoon **sugar**, 2 teaspoons **soy sauce**, 1 teaspoon **vinegar**, and ½ cup **regular-strength chicken broth**. Stir until thickened (about 1 minute).

SEAFOOD

Fillet of Sole with Asparagus

Bright green asparagus gives crunch and color to sole strips quickly sautéed with garlic.

2 teaspoons *each* cornstarch, soy sauce, and salad oil
¾ pound fillet of sole, cut in 1 by 3-inch strips
3 tablespoons salad oil
1 large clove garlic, minced or pressed
1 pound asparagus (tough ends removed), cut in ½-inch slanting slices
2 tablespoons regular-strength chicken broth or water

Mix together cornstarch, soy, and the 2 teaspoons salad oil. Stir in fish and mix until evenly coated.

Place wok over medium-high heat. When wok is hot, add 2 tablespoons of the oil. When oil is hot, add fish and gently stir-fry until golden (about 2 to 3 minutes); remove fish from wok and set aside.

Add remaining 1 tablespoon oil to wok. When oil is hot, add garlic and stir-fry for about 30 seconds. Add asparagus and stir-fry 30 seconds. Add chicken broth, cover and cook, stirring frequently, for about 3 to 4 minutes. Return fish to wok and stir-fry just to heat through. Makes 3 or 4 servings.

Sautéed Sesame Fish

Fish fillets are deliciously coated with a sesame-crumb mixture and served with fresh lemon-onion relish. Choose rockfish, halibut steaks, or fillets of lingcod.

Lemon-onion relish (directions follow)
2 pounds fish (suggestions above)
Salt and pepper
1 egg
2 tablespoons milk
½ cup fine dry bread crumbs
4 tablespoons sesame seed
About 2 tablespoons *each* salad oil and butter or margarine

Prepare lemon-onion relish and set aside.

Cut fish into serving-size pieces (about 2 by 3 inches). Sprinkle with salt and pepper. In a bowl, beat together egg and milk. In another bowl, mix together bread crumbs and sesame seed.

Dip fish into egg-milk mixture, then into crumb-seed mixture until fish is evenly coated on all sides.

Place a wok over medium-high heat. When wok is hot, add oil and butter. When butter has melted, add 2 pieces of fish at a time; gently turn fish as needed to brown, and cook until fish flakes easily when prodded in thickest portion with a fork (about 2 minutes). Remove fish from wok and keep warm. Repeat, using more oil and butter, if needed. Pass lemon-onion relish to spoon over. Makes 4 servings.

Lemon-onion relish. In a small bowl, combine 2 tablespoons *each* chopped **parsley** and freshly squeezed **lemon juice**, and ¼ cup finely chopped **green onion**.

Bright green edible-pod peas are quickly
stir-fried with colorful pink shrimp and water chestnuts.
The recipe is on page 24.

Scampi

We've developed a quick and easy version of classic Italian scampi using medium-size shrimp. Accompany with hot buttered noodles, rice, or spaghetti.

    3 tablespoons butter or margarine
    2 tablespoons salad oil
    1 tablespoon minced green onion
    4 to 5 cloves garlic, minced or pressed
    2 teaspoons lemon juice
    ¼ teaspoon salt
       About ¾ pound medium-size raw
          shrimp, shelled and deveined
    ¼ teaspoon grated lemon peel
    2 tablespoons minced parsley
       Dash liquid hot pepper seasoning
       Lemon wedges

Place wok over medium-high heat. When wok is hot, add butter and oil. When butter has melted, add onion, garlic, lemon juice, and salt; stir-fry until onion is limp (about 30 seconds). Turn heat to high, add shrimp, and stir-fry until shrimp turn pink (about 2 minutes). Stir in lemon peel, parsley, and hot pepper seasoning. Garnish with lemon wedges to squeeze over each serving. Makes 2 servings.

Edible-pod Peas with Shrimp

Pictured on page 23

When shelling the shrimp, you can leave the tails on for a decorative touch, if you like.

    1 teaspoon cornstarch
    ¼ teaspoon ground ginger
    2 tablespoons *each* soy sauce and dry
          sherry
    ½ cup regular-strength chicken broth
       About 3 tablespoons salad oil
    1 clove garlic, minced or pressed
    1 pound medium-size raw shrimp, shelled
          and deveined
    1½ cups (3 oz.) edible-pod peas, ends and
          strings removed, or 1 package (6 oz.)
          frozen edible-pod peas, thawed
    1 can (4 or 6 oz.) water chestnuts, drained
          and thinly sliced
    2 to 3 green onions, thinly sliced

Mix cornstarch and ginger; then blend in soy, sherry, and broth and set aside.

Place wok over high heat. When wok is hot, add oil. When oil is hot, add garlic and shrimp and stir-fry for about 1 minute. Add peas and stir-fry for about 2 minutes (30 seconds if frozen). Add water chestnuts and green onions; stir to mix. Add cornstarch mixture and stir until it boils and thickens (about 1 minute). Makes 4 servings.

Sausage Links and Shrimp Sauté

Chunks of brown-and-serve sausages cook quickly with shrimp and vegetables. Serve with a mixed fruit salad of grapes, apples, and pears.

       Cooking sauce (directions follow)
    1 package (8 oz.) brown-and-serve sausage
          links, cut in thirds
    1 medium-size onion, thinly sliced
       About ½ head cabbage, shredded
    1 can (4 to 6 oz.) water chestnuts,
          drained and sliced
       About ½ pound small cooked shrimp
       Hot cooked rice (optional)
       Soy sauce

Prepare cooking sauce and set aside.

Place wok over medium heat. When wok is hot, add sausage and stir-fry until browned (about 1 minute). Add onion and stir-fry until limp (about 2 minutes). Stir in cabbage, water chestnuts, and shrimp; cover and cook, stirring frequently, just until cabbage is wilted (about 3 minutes). Add cooking sauce and stir until it boils and thickens (about 1 minute). Serve with hot cooked rice, if desired; pass soy to serve over. Makes 3 or 4 servings.

Cooking sauce. Mix 2½ tablespoons **soy sauce,** 1½ tablespoons **dry sherry** or water, ½ teaspoon *each* **ground ginger** and **dry mustard,** 1 clove **garlic** (pressed or minced), and 2 teaspoons **cornstarch.**

Mizutaki...table-top cooking in an electric wok

Pictured on page 26

There are any number of wok-adaptable dishes that encourage guests to do the cooking themselves at the table. Here we offer mizutaki, borrowed from the Japanese. Serve with chopsticks if you like. One electric wok is adequate for six guests.

Leisurely, using your electric wok, guests cook morsels of meat and vegetables at the table. Then they fish the cooked food out of the simmering broth with little wire baskets on long handles, or with chopsticks or slotted spoons. Finally, they dip the food into individual containers of creamy mizutaki sauce, and eat with rice.

Here, an electric wok substitutes for a hot pot—a traditional Oriental charcoal-fired metal cooking pot with a center chimney surrounded by a moat that holds the broth for cooking.

In the kitchen, start heating the broth on the range. Add some of the vegetables that take longest to cook—cauliflower, carrots, broccoli. Then carefully transfer hot liquid into wok at the table and let guests add the ingredients they choose. Serve with rice.

Prepare mizutaki sauce and pour into 6 small bowls, one for each guest. Arrange vegetables and meat attractively in containers that you can take to the table.

Pour broth into a large pan. Place over medium-high heat, cover and bring to simmering. Add a few carrot, cauliflower, and broccoli pieces to get a head start on the cooking. Transfer to wok at the table and add a few pieces of meat and chicken. The food is ready to eat when vegetables are tender-crisp, meat is pale in color, and chicken is opaque.

Encourage guests to spoon foods of their choice into the simmering broth, adding mushrooms, spinach, and tofu last, if used. Dip cooked pieces into mizutaki sauce to eat.

Toward the end of the meal, ladle some of the cooking broth into the individual mizutaki sauce bowls, stirring it into the sauce left in bowls. Sip it like a soup. Makes 6 servings.

Mizutaki sauce (directions follow)
2 cans (47 oz. *each*) regular-strength chicken broth
1 pound carrots, cut in ¼-inch slanting slices
1 small head cauliflower, cut into small flowerets
1 bunch broccoli (about 1¼ lbs.), cut into small flowerets
1½ pounds lean boneless beef, pork, or lamb, cut in ¼-inch slanting slices
3 whole chicken breasts (about 1¼ lbs. *each*), skinned, boned, and cut into bite-size pieces
½ pound mushrooms, sliced ¼ inch thick
1 bunch (about ¾ lb.) spinach, stems removed
½ pound medium-firm tofu, cut in 1-inch cubes (optional)

Mizutaki sauce. In a blender, combine 1 **egg**, 2 tablespoons **rice wine vinegar** or white wine vinegar, ¼ teaspoon **dry mustard**, and ¼ cup **salad oil**; whirl until smooth. With blender motor on high, gradually add ¾ cup **salad oil** in a slow, steady stream. Whirl about 30 seconds more, then pour into a bowl. Stir in ⅓ cup **sour cream**, 2 tablespoons *each* **soy sauce** and **mirin** (rice wine) or dry sherry, and ⅓ cup **regular-strength beef broth** or chicken broth. Makes 1¼ cups.

*Cooking at the table in an electric wok is fun for guests.
Chicken, beef, and assorted vegetables
are cooked in broth for mizutaki. The recipe is on page 25.*

Shrimp-Vegetable Tumble

Pictured on front cover

Steamed rice is all you need to accompany this colorful entrée of shrimp and vegetables.

- 1 pound medium-size raw shrimp, shelled and deveined
- 1 tablespoon dry sherry
- ½ teaspoon salt
- 1 teaspoon cornstarch
  Cooking sauce (directions follow)
- 3 tablespoons salad oil
- 3 cloves garlic, minced or pressed
- 3 teaspoons chopped fresh ginger
- 2½ cups cauliflower flowerets, cut in ½-inch slices
- 2 medium-size carrots, cut in ½-inch slanting slices
- 4 tablespoons water
- 2½ cups small broccoli flowerets
- ½ pound asparagus (tough ends removed), cut in ½-inch slanting slices
- ¼ pound mushrooms, thinly sliced
- 5 green onions, cut in 1½-inch lengths

In a bowl, combine shrimp, sherry, salt, and cornstarch. Prepare cooking sauce and set aside.

Place wok on high heat. When wok is hot, add 1½ tablespoons of the oil. When oil begins to heat, add garlic and ginger. Stir once, add shrimp, and stir-fry until they turn pink (about 3 minutes). Remove from wok.

Heat remaining 1½ tablespoons oil. Add cauliflower and carrots and stir-fry for 1 minute. Add 2 tablespoons of the water; cover and cook, stirring occasionally, for 3 minutes. Stir in broccoli, asparagus, and 1 more tablespoon of the water. Cover and cook for 2 minutes. Stir in mushrooms, onions, and remaining 1 tablespoon water. Cover and cook for 1 minute.

Return shrimp to wok. Add cooking sauce and stir until it boils and thickens slightly (about 1 minute). Makes 4 to 6 servings.

Cooking sauce. Mix together ½ cup **chicken stock**, 2 tablespoons **soy sauce**, and 1 tablespoon **cornstarch.**

Sautéed Oysters with Basil

Oysters benefit from light cooking. They plump to succulence and release delicate juices when sautéed. If you buy your oysters in the shell, re-turn the cooked oysters to their shells for dramatic serving.

- 8 Eastern or 6 medium-size Pacific oysters (usually sold in jars)
  All-purpose flour
- 2 tablespoons butter or margarine
- ½ teaspoon dry basil
- 2 tablespoons dry white wine

If in shells, cut oysters free and remove. Gently pat oysters dry. Dredge in flour and shake off excess.

Place wok over medium-high heat. When wok is hot, add butter. When butter has melted, add oysters and sprinkle with basil. Stir-fry oysters gently for about 4 minutes. Arrange on a serving dish or place each oyster in a half shell; keep warm.

Add wine to wok and stir up browned particles. Spoon liquid over oysters. Makes 2 servings.

Chinese Scallops in Oyster Sauce

Bright green edible-pod peas and tender scallops are tossed quickly in a hot wok to mingle with rich oyster sauce. Buy oyster sauce in the Oriental section of your market.

- 2 tablespoons oyster sauce or soy sauce
- 2 teaspoons cornstarch
- 1 teaspoon soy sauce
- ¼ teaspoon sugar
- ½ pound scallops (thawed if frozen), well rinsed, drained, and sliced across the grain
- 2 tablespoons butter or margarine
- 1½ cups (3 oz.) edible-pod peas, ends and strings removed, or 1 package (6 oz.) frozen edible-pod peas, thawed
- ¼ cup chopped green onion
  Hot cooked rice

Combine oyster sauce, cornstarch, soy, and sugar. Stir scallops into oyster sauce mixture; set aside.

Place wok over medium heat. When wok is hot, add butter. When butter has melted, add peas and onion and stir-fry for 2 or 3 minutes or until vegetables are tender-crisp. (If using frozen pod peas, stir-fry for 30 seconds or until heated through.) Raise heat to high, add scallop mixture, and stir-fry for about 3 minutes or until scallops are just opaque throughout and sauce is slightly thickened. Spoon over hot cooked rice and serve immediately. Makes 4 servings.

Seafood Stroganoff

Salmon and shrimp complement each other in a tomato and sour cream sauce much like the sauce for beef stroganoff. It's an interesting combination to serve over rice, noodles, or green noodles.

    1   to 1½ pounds salmon fillets or steaks or
        fillets of Greenland turbot, thawed
        if frozen
    ¼   cup butter or margarine
    1   medium-size onion, thinly sliced
    ¼   pound mushrooms, thinly sliced
    1   can (about 14 oz.) pear-shaped
        tomatoes
    ½   teaspoon salt
    1   teaspoon Worcestershire
    1   tablespoon *each* lime juice and catsup
    ½   pound medium-size raw shrimp, shelled
        and deveined
    1   cup sour cream
    2   tablespoons all-purpose flour

Remove any bone or skin from fish and cut into bite-size pieces; set aside.

Place wok over medium-high heat. When wok is hot, add butter. When butter has melted, add onion and stir-fry until limp (about 2 minutes). Add mushrooms and stir-fry until limp (about 2 minutes). Add tomatoes (breaking up tomatoes with spatula), salt, Worcestershire, lime juice, and catsup. Cook, stirring until liquid is reduced to thickness of heavy cream. Stir in shrimp; cover and simmer for about 1 minute. Stir in fish and simmer for about 2 minutes. Blend sour cream

with flour until smooth; stir into fish mixture and cook, stirring, just to heat through and thicken (about 1 minute). Makes about 6 servings.

Crab Meat Patties

Use fresh, frozen, or canned Dungeness or king crab meat to make these little crab patties, then sauté them two at a time.

    1   pound (about 2 cups) crab meat or 2
        cans (7½ oz. *each*) crab meat, drained
   20   saltine crackers, crushed
    4   teaspoons Worcestershire
    ⅛   teaspoon liquid hot pepper seasoning
    3   tablespoons chopped parsley
   1½   teaspoons prepared mustard
    3   tablespoons mayonnaise
    1   egg, slightly beaten
    3   tablespoons butter or margarine
        Chopped parsley and lemon wedges

Flake crab into bowl with cracker crumbs. Add Worcestershire, hot pepper seasoning, parsley, mustard, and mayonnaise. Stir until blended. Stir in egg. Shape mixture with your hands into 8 flat patties.

Place wok over medium heat. When wok is hot, add 2 tablespoons of the butter. When butter has melted, add crab patties 2 or 3 at a time. Cook, turning until browned on both sides (about 6 minutes total). If needed, add remaining 1 tablespoon butter when you turn cakes. Garnish with parsley and lemon wedges. Makes 4 servings.

Fried Oysters with Eggs

Crisp-fried oysters rest on a bed of scrambled eggs. Accompany with English muffins.

    1   jar (10 oz.) medium-size Pacific oysters,
        drained and cut into bite-size pieces
    2   teaspoons soy sauce
    1   teaspoon minced fresh ginger root or ½
        teaspoon ground ginger
    6   eggs
    ¼   cup milk
    ½   teaspoon garlic salt
        Dash pepper
    2   tablespoons salad oil
    1   tablespoon butter or margarine
        Sliced green onion (optional)

Mix together oysters, soy, and ginger; set aside.

Beat eggs lightly with milk, garlic salt, and pepper; set aside.

Place wok over high heat. When wok is hot, add oil. When oil is hot, add oyster mixture. Stir-fry for 1 minute or until oysters begin to brown slightly. Remove from wok and set aside.

Clean and dry wok and return to medium-low heat. When wok is hot, add butter. When butter has melted, add egg mixture. Cook eggs, gently lifting cooked portion with spatula to allow uncooked portion to flow underneath. When eggs are almost set but creamy, return oysters to wok, and mix in gently until eggs are set to your liking. Garnish with green onion, if desired. Makes 4 to 6 servings.

POULTRY

Chicken with Fresh Pears

Strips of chicken cook with pears. Garnish with a sprinkling of roasted cashews.

    Cooking sauce (directions follow)
 3 tablespoons salad oil
 2 cloves garlic, minced or pressed
 2 pounds chicken breasts, skinned,
        boned, and cut in bite-size pieces
 2 stalks celery, thinly sliced
 3 green onions, cut in 2-inch pieces
 1 can (6 oz.) sliced bamboo shoots,
        drained
 2 medium-size pears (unpeeled),
        quartered, cored, and cut in ½-inch-
        wide slices
 1 package (6 oz.) frozen edible-pod
        peas, thawed
 ½ cup salted roasted cashews

Prepare cooking sauce and set aside.

Place wok over high heat. When wok is hot, add 1 tablespoon of the oil. When oil is hot, add the garlic and half the chicken; stir-fry until chicken is opaque (about 3 minutes). Remove from pan and set aside. Repeat with remaining chicken, adding another tablespoon oil. Reheat wok and add the remaining 1 tablespoon oil. When oil is hot, add celery, onion, and bamboo shoots; stir-fry for about 3 minutes. Add pears, peas, chicken, and cooking sauce; stir until it boils and thickens (about 1 minute). Garnish with cashews. Makes 6 servings.

Cooking sauce. Mix 4 teaspoons **cornstarch**, 1 teaspoon **sugar**, 2 teaspoons minced **fresh ginger root**, ¾ teaspoon **salt**, 2 tablespoons *each* **soy sauce** and **dry sherry**, and ¾ cup **regular-strength chicken broth**.

Vietnamese Chicken Salad

Unlike most chicken salads, which call for leftover cooked meat, this one begins with seasoned slivers of uncooked chicken breast that you quickly stir-fry and then chill. Combine the chilled chicken with a lemony dressing and crisp shreds of cabbage and green onion for a luncheon entrée.

 2   green onions
 1½ pounds chicken breasts, skinned,
        boned, and cut into matchstick-
        size strips
 ½   teaspoon minced fresh ginger root
 1   teaspoon salt
 ½   teaspoon pepper
 4   tablespoons salad oil
 3   tablespoons lemon juice
 ½   teaspoon sugar
 3   cups finely shredded cabbage

Cut green tops of onions in 2-inch pieces, then cut each piece lengthwise into thin strips; set aside. Finely chop white part of onions. Combine chopped onion, chicken, ginger, ½ teaspoon of the salt, and ¼ teaspoon of the pepper.

Place wok on high heat. When wok is hot, add 2 tablespoons of the oil. When oil is hot, add chicken mixture. Stir-fry until chicken is opaque (about 3 minutes); remove chicken from wok; cool, cover, and chill.

Stir together lemon juice, sugar, and remaining 2 tablespoons oil, ½ teaspoon salt, and ¼ teaspoon pepper. Just before serving, mix together chilled chicken, lemon dressing, cabbage, and onion strips. Makes 2 servings.

Cashew Chicken for Two

When there are just the two of you, try this quick-to-the-table dish full of vegetables topped with roasted cashews.

(Continued on next page)

    1 teaspoon cornstarch
    ½ cup regular-strength chicken broth
    1 tablespoon *each* cornstarch and
        soy sauce
    1 pound chicken breast, skinned, boned,
        and cut in matchstick-size pieces
      About 4 tablespoons salad oil
    1 stalk celery, thinly sliced
    ¼ pound green beans, cut in ½-inch
        slanting slices
    1 large carrot, cut in ¼-inch slanting slices
    1 small onion, cut in half, then in ¼-inch
        slices
    1 clove garlic, minced or pressed
    2 tablespoons water
    ⅓ cup roasted cashews

Mix the 1 teaspoon cornstarch with chicken broth; set aside.

Combine the 1 tablespoon cornstarch, soy, and chicken. Mix well to coat chicken thoroughly; set aside.

Place wok on high heat. When wok is hot, add 2 tablespoons of the oil. When oil is hot, add chicken mixture. Stir-fry until chicken is opaque (about 3 minutes); remove chicken from wok and set aside.

Add remaining 2 tablespoons oil to wok. When oil is hot, add celery, beans, carrot, onion, and garlic. Stir-fry for 1 minute. Add water, cover and cook for 3 minutes or until vegetables are just tender-crisp.

Return chicken and chicken broth mixture to pan. Stir until liquid boils and thickens (about 1 minute). Stir in most of the cashews. Garnish with remaining cashews. Makes 2 servings.

Watercress Chicken with Mushrooms

This chicken stir-fry will serve four, if served with two or three other dishes.

    ½ pound (about 2 bunches) watercress
      Cooking sauce (directions follow)
    2 pounds chicken breasts, skinned,
        boned, and cut in 1-inch squares
    2 cloves garlic, minced or pressed
    ¼ teaspoon *each* pepper and ground ginger
    2 or 3 teaspoons sesame seed (optional)
    5 tablespoons salad oil
    ½ pound mushrooms, sliced

Pluck green watercress leaves from stems and lightly pack in cup. Coarsely chop the thinnest stems and add to leaves; discard thick stems. (You should have about 4 cups lightly packed watercress.)

Prepare cooking sauce and set aside. Season chicken with garlic, pepper, and ginger.

Place wok on medium heat. When wok is hot, add sesame seed, if desired, and stir until golden (about 30 seconds); remove from wok and set aside. Turn heat to high and add 2 tablespoons of the oil to wok. When oil is hot, add half the chicken and stir-fry just until chicken is opaque (about 3 minutes). Remove chicken from wok and set aside. Repeat, using 1 more tablespoon oil and remaining chicken.

Add remaining 2 tablespoons oil to wok. When oil is hot, add mushrooms and stir-fry for about 3 minutes.

Add watercress and toasted sesame seed, if used; stir-fry for about 30 seconds.

Add chicken and cooking sauce. Stir until sauce boils and thickens (about 1 minute). Makes 3 or 4 servings.

Cooking sauce. Mix together 1 teaspoon **brown sugar**, 1 teaspoon **cornstarch**, 1 tablespoon **dry sherry**, and 2½ tablespoons **soy sauce**.

Hot and Sour Chicken

From the Hunan area of China comes hot and sour chicken. The hot comes from crushed red pepper, the sour from white wine vinegar. The fermented black beans in this recipe can be found in Oriental food stores. Serve the dish with translucent bean threads (page 9) or hot cooked rice, if you like.

      Cooking sauce (directions follow)
    2 teaspoons *each* cornstarch, dry sherry,
        and salad oil
    ¼ teaspoon *each* salt and pepper
    1¼ pounds chicken breasts, skinned,
        boned, and cut in ¾-inch cubes
    3 tablespoons salad oil
    1 tablespoon finely chopped garlic
    2 teaspoons finely chopped fresh ginger
        root or 1 teaspoon ground ginger
    1 tablespoon fermented black beans,
        rinsed and dried
    1 small green pepper, seeded and cut in
        1-inch squares
    1 medium-size carrot, thinly sliced
    1 can (about 8 oz.) sliced bamboo shoots,
        drained
    1 tablespoon water

Prepare cooking sauce and set aside.

Mix together cornstarch, sherry, the 2 teaspoons oil, and salt and pepper. Add chicken cubes and toss; set aside.

(Continued on page 32)

All-American sloppy Joes and corn-on-the-cob
were both prepared in a wok. Stir-fried quick sloppy Joes recipe
is on page 37; steamed corn, page 66.

Place wok over high heat. When wok is hot, add 2 tablespoons of the oil. When oil is hot, add chicken mixture. Stir-fry for about 2 minutes. Add garlic, ginger, and black beans. Stir-fry until chicken is lightly browned (about 2 minutes more). Remove chicken mixture and set aside.

Reheat wok and add the remaining 1 tablespoon oil. When oil is hot, add green pepper, carrot, bamboo shoots, and water. Stir-fry for 2 minutes. Return chicken mixture to wok, add cooking sauce, and stir until it boils and thickens (about 1 minute). Makes 2 or 3 servings.

Cooking sauce. Mix together 2 teaspoons **cornstarch**, ½ teaspoon *each* **crushed red pepper** and **salad oil**, 2 tablespoons **soy sauce**, 2½ tablespoons **white wine vinegar**, and ½ cup **regular-strength chicken broth**.

about 1 minute or until tender-crisp. Return chicken to wok. Add sweet and sour sauce and pineapple. Stir until liquid boils and thickens (about 1 minute).

Spoon equal portions of chicken mixture into each of the 4 pineapple shells; mound the mixture at one end and spoon in equal portions of rice alongside. Pass any extra chicken in bowl. Garnish with sprigs of coriander, if desired. Makes 4 servings.

Sweet and sour sauce. Stir together 4 teaspoons **cornstarch**, ¼ cup *each* **sugar** and **wine vinegar**, 2 tablespoons minced fresh **coriander** (cilantro) or 1½ teaspoons dry cilantro leaves, 2 tablespoons **catsup**, 1 tablespoon *each* **soy sauce** and **dry sherry**, ½ teaspoon **ground ginger**, ¼ teaspoon *each* **salt** and **crushed red pepper**, and ¼ cup **regular-strength chicken broth**.

Sweet and Sour Chicken in a Pineapple Shell

Pineapple shells make inventive serving containers for this handsome salad entrée. Fill them with sweet and sour pineapple chunks, chicken, and rice.

> 2 small pineapples
> Sweet and sour sauce (directions follow)
> 3 tablespoons salad oil
> 1¾ pounds chicken breasts, skinned, boned, and cut in ½ by 2-inch strips
> 1 clove garlic, minced or pressed
> 1 medium-size onion, thinly sliced
> 1 medium-size green pepper, seeded and cut in thin strips
> About 4 cups hot cooked rice
> Fresh coriander sprigs (cilantro or Chinese parsley), optional

Cut pineapples in half lengthwise, cutting through crowns. With a curved, serrated knife, cut fruit from rinds, leaving shells intact; turn shells upside down to drain. Trim away cores from fruit, then cut fruit in about ½-inch-thick chunks. You'll need 3 cups; reserve any remaining fruit for another use.

Just before cooking, drain the 3 cups pineapple chunks; reserve juice for other use.

Prepare sweet and sour sauce and set aside.

Place wok over high heat. When wok is hot, add 2 tablespoons of the oil. When oil is hot, add chicken and garlic; stir-fry until chicken is opaque (about 4 minutes); remove from wok and set aside.

Add remaining 1 tablespoon oil to wok. When oil is hot, add onion and green pepper. Stir-fry for

Chicken with Basil

An inspiration from Thailand, this chicken dish is highly seasoned with basil and green chiles.

> 3 or 4 tablespoons seeded and finely chopped, canned California green chiles
> 2 tablespoons soy sauce
> 1 teaspoon *each* sugar and vinegar
> ½ cup chopped fresh basil or 2 tablespoons dried basil
> 1 teaspoon chopped fresh mint or ¼ teaspoon dry mint
> ½ teaspoon cornstarch
> About 3 tablespoons salad oil
> 1 clove garlic, minced or pressed
> 2 pounds chicken breasts, skinned, boned, and cut in ¼ by 2-inch strips
> 1 large onion, cut in ¼-inch slices

Mix together chiles, soy, sugar, vinegar, basil, mint, and cornstarch; set aside.

Place wok on high heat. When wok is hot, add 1½ tablespoons of the oil. When oil is hot, add garlic and half the chicken; stir-fry until chicken is opaque (about 3 minutes); remove from wok and set aside. Repeat with remaining chicken, adding oil as needed. Reheat wok and add 1 table-

(Continued on page 34)

Camping with a wok

Have you considered taking your wok with you when you go camping? It may be the only major cooking utensil you'll need.

A wok works well cradled over an open fire between a few large rocks. It also cooks efficiently over a gas or propane-fueled camp stove, charcoal-heated hibachi, small portable barbecue, and standard park fireplace.

In your wok, you can scramble eggs, cook bacon, fry trout or hamburgers, or stir-fry any recipe from this book.

To cook over an open fire, arrange three or four large rocks in a ring to cradle the wok (wok bottom should be about 6 inches above ground). Start a little fire and wait until it's burning well—use small kindling wood for quick, hot cooking and larger pieces for slower cooking and steaming.

For wood-burning park fireplaces, set the wok directly on the grill or stove top. To compensate for the greater distance between the fire and the bottom of the wok, build as big a fire as necessary.

Use portable gas or propane-fueled camp stoves the same way you would use a gas range at home. For most cooking, set the wok directly on the burner; for steaming, set the wok on its ring stand over the burner. With a very small unit, you may need to drop back the stove lid and wind shields in order to center the wok over a burner.

With a hibachi or small portable barbecue, place a single layer of charcoal briquets in the bottom for fast cooking. With charcoal in place, position the wok for cooking. For high heat, set the wok directly on the hibachi (without grill)—the wok should be not more than ½ inch above the coals, but not touching. (If coals are too low, add briquets; if too high, replace grill and set the wok on top.)

For lower heat, set the wok ring stand on top of the grill and set the wok in the ring stand; the bottom of the wok should be about 1½ inches above the coals. After making these adjustments, start the fire and let it burn until the coals are covered with gray ash.

Hamburgers with Onion Rings

Mix 1 pound **lean ground beef** with 1 teaspoon **garlic salt,** 1 tablespoon **instant minced onion,** and ¼ teaspoon **pepper.** Form 4 patties, each about ½ inch thick. Place wok over fire. When wok is hot, lay patties near bottom of wok. Also place 4 **English muffin halves,** cut sides down, in wok slightly above patties. Cook patties to desired doneness (about 5 minutes on each side for medium-rare). Place each on a muffin half. Top with **canned fried onion rings.** Makes 4 servings.

Ham and Zucchini Stir-fry

Stir together ¼ cup **regular-strength chicken broth,** 1 tablespoon **soy sauce,** 1 tablespoon **dry sherry** (optional), 1 clove **garlic** (minced or pressed), ½ teaspoon **grated fresh ginger root** or ¼ teaspoon ground ginger, 1 tablespoon **sugar,** ¼ teaspoon **salt,** and 1 teaspoon **cornstarch.**

Cut ½ pound **cooked ham** or leftover meat into ¼-inch-thick slices, then into 2-inch strips. Cut 1 large **carrot** and 1 large **zucchini** into ¼-inch-thick slices. Slice 1 large **onion** (optional).

Place wok over high heat. When wok is hot, add 3 tablespoons **salad oil.** When oil is hot, add ham and stir-fry until lightly browned (about 1 minute). Add carrot, zucchini, onion, and 1 tablespoon water. Stir-fry 1 minute. Cover and cook, stirring frequently, for 2 minutes. Pour in chicken broth mixture. Cook, stirring, until mixture boils and thickens. Makes 2 servings.

Steamed Trout and Vegetables

Slice as thinly as possible 1 large **onion,** 2 stalks **celery,** and 2 small **carrots.** Melt ¼ cup **butter** or margarine in an 8 or 9-inch foil pan; stir in ½ teaspoon *each* **salt** and **Italian seasoning** (or thyme leaves). Dip 2 cleaned **trout** into butter mixture to coat.

Stir vegetables into butter mixture and lay fish on top. Place pan on a rack or ring stand over simmering water in wok; lightly cover fish with foil. Cover wok and steam for about 15 minutes or until fish flakes easily when prodded in thickest portion with a fork. Makes 2 servings.

spoon oil. Add onion and stir-fry until limp (about 1 minute). Add chile mixture and return chicken to wok; stir until sauce boils and thickens slightly (about 1 minute). Makes 3 or 4 servings.

Slivered Chicken and Walnuts

In this meal for two, you could use cashews or peanuts instead of walnuts.

> Cooking sauce (directions follow)
> 1 pound chicken breast, skinned, boned, and cut in matchstick-size pieces
> 1 tablespoon soy sauce
> 1 teaspoon cornstarch
> 3 tablespoons salad oil
> ½ cup walnut halves
> 1 medium-size green pepper, seeded and cut into 1-inch squares
> ½ teaspoon finely minced fresh ginger root

Prepare cooking sauce and set aside.

Mix chicken pieces with soy and cornstarch and set aside.

Place wok over medium-high heat. When wok is hot, add oil. When oil is hot, add walnuts and stir-fry until brown (about 1 minute); remove walnuts with a slotted spoon and set aside. Add chicken to oil and stir-fry until chicken is opaque (about 3 minutes); remove from wok and set aside.

Add green pepper and ginger and stir-fry until pepper is tender-crisp (about 1 minute). Add chicken and cooking sauce, stirring until it boils and thickens (about 1 minute). Stir in walnuts. Makes 2 servings.

Cooking sauce. Blend ½ teaspoon **cornstarch,** dash **liquid hot pepper seasoning,** ¾ teaspoon *each* **sugar** and **wine vinegar,** 1 teaspoon **dry sherry** or water, and 1 tablespoon **soy sauce.**

Chicken with Eggplant

Small dried hot chile peppers add life to the mild-tasting eggplant in this dish. For a less spicy flavor, use only one chile.

> 1 small eggplant (about 1 lb.), cut in ¾ by 3-inch strips
> Boiling water
> 1 tablespoon cornstarch
> 2 tablespoons soy sauce
> 1 to 1¼ pounds chicken breasts or thighs, skinned, boned, and cut in ½ by 2-inch strips
> 4 tablespoons salad oil
> 1 or 2 small, dry, hot chile peppers, split in half and seeded
> 1 clove garlic, minced or pressed
> 1 teaspoon grated fresh ginger root or ½ teaspoon ground ginger
> 4 tablespoons water
> 1 can (4 or 6 oz.) water chestnuts, drained and sliced
> 3 tablespoons regular-strength chicken broth or water
> 1 tablespoon dry sherry
> Sliced green onions or chopped parsley

Place eggplant in a bowl and pour over boiling water to cover. Let stand about 7 minutes; drain and pat dry.

Combine cornstarch with soy and chicken; mix well to coat chicken thoroughly; set aside.

Place wok on high heat. When wok is hot, add oil. When oil is hot, add chiles. When chiles begin to brown, remove from wok with wire skimmer and discard. Add garlic, ginger, eggplant, and 2 tablespoons of the water. Stir-fry for about 2 minutes. Add remaining 2 tablespoons water, cover, and steam, stirring frequently, for 10 minutes, or until eggplant is tender; remove from wok.

Add chicken and water chestnuts; stir-fry until chicken is opaque (about 2 minutes). Add chicken broth, sherry, and eggplant; cook for about 1 minute. Sprinkle with green onion, if desired. Makes 4 servings.

Chicken Cacciatore

A wok in an Italian kitchen may seem incongruous, but Italy's chicken cacciatore can be easily cooked in a wok to serve over a bed of spaghetti.

1 can (6 oz.) tomato paste
¾ cup dry white wine
½ teaspoon *each* oregano leaves and dry basil
½ teaspoon salt
¼ teaspoon thyme leaves
Dash pepper
About 3 tablespoons salad oil
2½ pounds chicken breasts, skinned, boned, and cut into bite-size pieces
1 large onion, thinly sliced and separated into rings
1 green pepper, seeded and cut into ½-inch squares
¼ pound mushrooms, thinly sliced
Hot spaghetti
Grated Parmesan cheese

Stir together tomato paste, white wine, oregano, basil, salt, thyme, and pepper; set aside.

Place wok over high heat. When wok is hot,

add 1 tablespoon of the oil. When oil is hot, add half the chicken and stir-fry until chicken is opaque (about 3 minutes); remove chicken from wok and keep warm. Repeat with remaining chicken, adding oil as needed.

Reheat wok and add 1 tablespoon oil. When oil is hot, add onion and stir-fry until limp (about 2 minutes). Add green pepper and mushrooms and stir-fry for about 2 minutes or until vegetables are limp.

Return chicken to wok. Pour in tomato mixture; stir to heat through. Spoon over hot spaghetti. Pass grated Parmesan cheese to spoon over. Makes 4 or 5 servings.

Almond Turkey with Peas

This supper dish takes advantage of any leftover turkey or chicken. Another time, you might make the same entrée with cold cooked beef or pork, or with baked ham.

¼ cup slivered almonds
2 tablespoons butter or margarine
½ pound mushrooms, sliced
1 package (10 oz.) frozen petite peas, thawed
¼ pound fresh edible-pod peas, ends and strings removed, or 1 package (6 oz.) frozen edible-pod peas, thawed
¾ cup regular-strength chicken broth
1 can (4 to 6 oz.) water-chestnuts, drained and thinly sliced
2 or 3 cups cold cooked turkey or chicken, cut in bite-size pieces
⅓ cup thinly sliced green onion
4 teaspoons cornstarch
1 tablespoon soy sauce

Spread almonds in a shallow pan; toast in a 350° oven until lightly browned (about 5 minutes); set aside.

Place wok on medium heat. When wok is hot, add butter. When butter has melted, add mushrooms and stir-fry until golden and limp (about 3 minutes). Add peas, pod peas, and ½ cup of the broth; stir-fry for about 2 minutes (30 seconds if using frozen pod peas) or until peas are heated through. Add water chestnuts, turkey, and onion; stir-fry for about 1 minute. Combine cornstarch, soy, and remaining ¼ cup chicken broth; add to turkey mixture and stir and cook until it boils and thickens (about 1 minute).

Garnish with toasted almonds. Makes 4 to 6 servings.

MEATS

Beef and Broccoli Chow Mein

The Chinese word "chow" describes any stir-fried dish, while "mein" refers to thin, round Chinese noodles. Here these noodles are fried in small patties and served with beef and broccoli, but you could use them with other combinations.

- 2 quarts salted water
- 5 to 6 ounces dried Chinese noodles ("mein")
  About ½ cup salad oil
  Cooking sauce (directions follow)
- 1 pound boneless lean beef (flank or round steak)
- 2 tablespoons soy sauce
- 1 clove garlic, minced or pressed
- ¾ pound broccoli, cut into small flowerets, with stems cut in ¼-inch-thick slices
- 2 tablespoons water

In a 3-quart pan, bring salted water to boil. Place noodles in boiling water. Cook, uncovered, for 7 to 10 minutes; drain, rinse with cold water, and drain again thoroughly. Stir in 1 tablespoon of the oil; set aside.

Meanwhile, prepare cooking sauce and set aside.

Cut beef with the grain in 1½-inch wide strips. Cut each strip across the grain in ¼-inch-thick slanting slices. Mix beef with soy and garlic. Let stand for 15 minutes to marinate.

Place wok over medium heat. When wok is hot, add ¼ cup oil. When oil is hot, add noodles (use two spoons or tongs to make little mounds). Fry noodles gently until lightly browned on both sides (about 10 minutes total); remove from wok and set aside.

Turn heat to high. Add 1 tablespoon of the oil to wok. When oil is hot, add half the meat mixture. Stir-fry until lightly browned (about 2 minutes); remove meat from wok. Repeat, using 1 more tablespoon oil and remaining meat.

Add 2 more tablespoons oil to wok. When oil is hot, add broccoli and stir-fry for about 1 minute. Add water, cover, and cook, stirring frequently, for 3 minutes or until tender-crisp. Add cooking sauce, meat, and stir until it boils and thickens (about 1 minute). Pour over noodles. Makes 3 servings.

Cooking sauce. Mix together 1½ tablespoons **cornstarch**, ¼ teaspoon **ground ginger**, a dash **cayenne**, 2 tablespoons **dry sherry**, and 1¼ cups **regular-strength beef broth.**

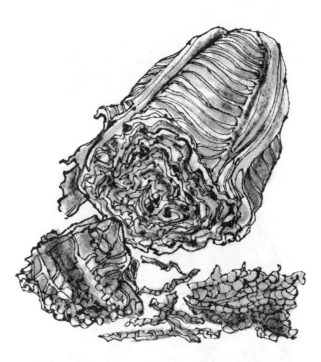

Beef with Chinese Cabbage

For an interesting vegetable variation, try Chinese cabbage, also known as celery cabbage or napa cabbage. Its curly leaves stay crisp when stir-fried with thin beef slices. When Chinese cabbage isn't available, though, feel free to use regular cabbage.

- ½ to ¾ pound boneless lean beef (sirloin, top round, or flank)
- 1 teaspoon cornstarch
- 1 tablespoon soy sauce
- ½ teaspoon minced fresh ginger root
  Cooking sauce (directions follow)
- ½ small head (about ¾ lb.) Chinese cabbage or regular cabbage
- 4 tablespoons salad oil
- 1 clove garlic, minced or pressed
- 1 medium-size green or red bell pepper, seeded and cut in 1-inch squares
- 2 green onions, thinly sliced

Cut beef with the grain in 1½-inch-wide strips. Cut each strip across the grain in ⅛-inch-thick slanting slices.

Combine cornstarch, soy, ginger, and beef, mixing to coat meat well. Let stand for 10 minutes.

Prepare cooking sauce and set aside.

Cut cabbage crosswise in ¾-inch slices (or regular cabbage in ¾-inch wedges).

Place wok over high heat. When wok is hot, add 2 tablespoons of the oil. When oil is hot, add meat mixture. Stir-fry until browned (about 2 minutes); set aside.

Add remaining 2 tablespoons oil. When oil is hot, add garlic and bell pepper. Stir-fry for about

30 seconds. Add cabbage and stir-fry for about 2 minutes or until cabbage is tender-crisp and bright green. Return meat to wok. Add cooking sauce and stir until it boils and thickens (about 1 minute). Mix in green onion. Makes 2 servings.

Cooking sauce. Mix together 1 tablespoon *each* **cornstarch** and **sugar**, ½ cup **regular-strength beef broth**, 1 tablespoon **soy sauce** or oyster sauce, and 1 tablespoon **dry sherry** or white wine.

Curried Meatballs

A diner's delight, these meatballs in their curry sauce can be garnished with coconut, cashews, cucumbers, and pineapple tidbits.

    1½ pounds lean ground beef
     1 tablespoon salad oil
     1 large onion, finely chopped
     1 teaspoon salt
     1 tablespoon curry powder
     1 can (14 oz.) regular-strength beef broth
    1½ tablespoons cornstarch
     1 tablespoon lemon juice
        About 2½ cups hot cooked rice
        Assorted condiments
          (suggestions follow)

Shape beef into bite-size meatballs (about 1-inch diameter); set aside.

Place wok over medium-high heat. When wok is hot, add oil. When oil is hot, add a few meatballs at a time and cook, stirring occasionally, until browned on all sides; set aside. Drain off all but 1 tablespoon drippings. Add onion and stir-fry until limp (about 1 minute). Add salt and curry powder; stir for about 30 seconds. Blend broth with cornstarch and pour into wok; bring to a boil. Cook, stirring, until thickened (about 1 minute); stir in lemon juice. Return meatballs and heat through. Serve over hot rice with assorted condiments. Makes 4 to 6 servings.

Assorted condiments. Place in individual bowls **flaked coconut; salted cashews,** chopped; chopped **cucumber; pineapple tidbits,** drained; chopped hard-cooked **egg;** and crumbled **bacon.**

Quick Sloppy Joes

Pictured on page 31

Pickle relish gives a sweet, spicy flavor to this version of a sloppy Joe topped with sour cream and avocado. Serve the ground beef mixture over regular hamburger or sourdough buns. Corn-on-the-cob makes a good eat-with-your-fingers companion.

    ½ teaspoon salt
     1 pound lean ground beef
     1 medium-size onion, chopped
    ¼ teaspoon pepper
     1 can (6 oz.) tomato paste
    ⅔ cup water
    ½ cup sweet pickle relish
     4 hamburger or sourdough buns, split
          and toasted
        Sour cream
        Avocado slices

Mix together salt and ground beef. Place wok over medium-high heat. When wok is hot, crumble in beef. Add onion and stir-fry until meat is browned and onion is limp (about 5 minutes). Spoon off and discard any fat.

Stir in pepper, tomato paste, water, and pickle relish. Stir for about 1 minute or until heated through. Spoon meat mixture over toasted buns. Top each with a sour cream dollop and an avocado slice. Makes 4 servings.

How to estimate servings for a Chinese dinner

A traditional Chinese-style dinner would offer many different main dishes served along with steamed rice. If you want to have such a meal at home, you may be puzzled as to how much food to prepare and how to judge how many guests each dish will serve.

Here is a simple guideline: add the pounds of boneless meat, poultry, and seafood in all the main dishes you plan to serve. Then allow a total of ¼ to ⅓ pound of meat, poultry, and seafood for each person.

In other words, if the total weight of all the meat, poultry, and seafood in your dishes is 1 pound, the dishes will serve 3 or 4 people. If the total weight is 2 pounds, they will serve 6 to 8 people, and so on.

The cook's discovery: tofu

Fresh soybean cake (tofu) is an unknown quantity to many cooks. Even those who come across the little plastic tubs of tofu in the produce section of the supermarket may not recognize it or know what to do with it.

Tofu is made from ground soybeans and has a tender, porous texture and bland taste—qualities that make it adaptable to all kinds of dishes, since it readily assumes the flavors of any ingredients you use with it. A nutritious food, tofu is high in protein, B vitamins, and calcium, but low in fat.

Here we offer general information on buying, using, and storing tofu, along with a recipe. You will also find tofu used in numerous recipes throughout this book.

How to buy tofu

Fresh tofu is sold in various stages of firmness, sometimes with only the Oriental name printed on the label. Here's a list of the most available forms of tofu.

Soft tofu. This very soft curd, also labeled kinugoshi, is packed with a little water to maintain freshness. It is frequently eaten cold with soy sauce, sliced green onions, and sesame seed. It can be diced and added to soup.

Medium-firm tofu. The curd is poured into trays, where it is drained of excess liquid and compressed. Frequently called Japanese-style tofu, it is sold in blocks weighing about 1 pound and packed in water. It is often preferred for stir-fry dishes.

Hard tofu. Drained and compressed, this tofu is sold in slices packed in water. It's one of the easiest forms of tofu to handle since it holds its shape well. It is also called Chinese-style tofu or bean cake.

Deep-fried tofu puffs are highly compressed curd fried in oil until puffy and hollow. They are available packed dry in plastic bags or tubs.

How to use and store tofu

Water-packed styles of tofu should always be drained before they're used. To do this, gently turn tofu into a colander and allow it to drain for about 20 minutes. To store leftover tofu, add enough fresh water to cover; then wrap airtight and refrigerate up to 10 days, changing the water every day to keep it fresh. Do not freeze. Tofu will smell sour if it has deteriorated.

Deep-fried tofu puffs, because they are already cooked, can be frozen up to a month if they are well wrapped. When refrigerated, they will keep for about 2 weeks.

Shrimp and Tofu Stir-fry

Cut the fresh soybean cake in cubes to stir-fry with the shrimp and onion mixture.

> Cooking sauce (directions follow)
> 4 tablespoons salad oil
> 1 clove garlic, minced or pressed
> ½ teaspoon grated fresh ginger root or ¼ teaspoon ground ginger
> 1 pound medium-size raw shrimp, shelled and deveined
> 1 medium-size onion, cut in ¼-inch-thick slices
> About 1 pound medium-firm tofu, drained and cut in 1-inch cubes
> 1 package (10 oz.) frozen peas, thawed

Prepare cooking sauce and set aside.

Place wok over high heat. When wok is hot, add 2 tablespoons of the oil. When oil is hot, add garlic, ginger, shrimp, and onion. Stir-fry until shrimp are pink (about 3 minutes). Remove shrimp mixture from wok and set aside.

Add the remaining 2 tablespoons oil to wok. When oil is hot, add tofu and peas. Stir-fry gently for about 2 minutes or until tofu is heated through. Return shrimp to wok, add cooking sauce, and stir-fry gently until sauce boils and thickens (about 1 minute). Makes 4 servings.

Cooking sauce. Stir together 1 tablespoon **cornstarch**, ½ teaspoon **salt**, and ⅛ teaspoon **pepper**. Blend in 2 tablespoons *each* **soy sauce** and **dry sherry**, and ⅓ cup **regular-strength chicken broth**.

Ginger Beef

As you might guess, lots of chopped fresh ginger deliciously flavors the thin steak strips in ginger beef.

    ¼ cup regular-strength beef broth
    1½ tablespoons soy sauce
    2 teaspoons dry sherry
    1 teaspoon sugar
    1½ pounds boneless beef sirloin
    2 tablespoons salad oil
    1 small clove garlic, minced or pressed
    2 tablespoons chopped fresh ginger root
    3 green onions, cut into ½-inch-wide
         slanting slices
    1 tablespoon *each* cornstarch and water

Combine broth, soy, sherry, and sugar; set aside.

Cut beef with the grain into 1½-inch-wide strips. Cut each strip across the grain in ⅛-inch-thick slanting slices.

Place wok over medium-high heat. When wok is hot, add 1 tablespoon of the oil. When oil is hot, add garlic and ginger. Stir-fry for about 30 seconds. Turn heat to high. Add half the beef and onion and stir-fry until meat is lightly browned (about 2 minutes); remove from wok. Repeat, using remaining 1 tablespoon oil, beef, and onion. Return cooked meat to wok. Pour in broth mixture; cover and simmer for 3 minutes. Mix cornstarch with water and gradually stir into wok. Cook until slightly thickened, stirring to coat meat (about 1 minute). Makes 4 to 6 servings.

Ground Beef with Rice and Vegetables

Leftover rice is delicious stir-fried with ground beef and other vegetables you may have on hand.

    ½ pound ground beef or ground lamb
    1 small onion, finely chopped
    1 clove garlic, minced or pressed
    1 small green pepper, seeded and diced
    4 or 5 fresh mushrooms, sliced ¼ inch thick
         About 2 tablespoons salad oil
    1 cup cooked rice
    1 cup frozen peas, thawed, or cooked
         green beans, carrots, or zucchini
    6 cherry tomatoes, halved
    2 tablespoons soy sauce
         About ¼ cup sliced or chopped almonds
         (optional)

Place wok over high heat. When wok is hot, crumble in beef and stir-fry until lightly browned (about 2 minutes). Remove beef and set aside. Discard all but 1 tablespoon drippings. Add onion and garlic and stir-fry for about 30 seconds. Add green pepper and mushrooms and stir-fry for about 2 minutes or until vegetables are tender-crisp. Remove from wok and set aside.

If needed, add enough oil to make about 2 tablespoons in wok. When oil is hot, add rice and stir-fry until it starts to brown. Stir in peas, meat, tomatoes, mushroom mixture, and soy. Stir-fry until heated through. Sprinkle with almonds, if desired. Makes 2 servings.

Ground Beef Garden Sauté

You can use green beans, zucchini, or carrots for the vegetables in this stir-fry. It's a good way to stretch a pound of ground beef.

    ⅓ cup slivered almonds
    4 eggs
    1 tablespoon soy sauce
    1 teaspoon ground ginger
    ½ teaspoon dry mustard
    ⅛ teaspoon pepper
    1 tablespoon salad oil
    ½ pound green beans, cut in 1-inch lengths
    2 tablespoons water
    1 pound lean ground beef
    1 medium-size onion, chopped
    2 cloves garlic, minced or pressed

(Continued on next page)

Spread almonds in a shallow baking pan. Toast in a 325° oven until lightly browned (about 10 minutes); set aside.

Beat together eggs, soy, ginger, mustard, and pepper; set aside.

Place wok over high heat. When wok is hot, add oil. When oil is hot, add beans and stir-fry 1 minute. Add water, cover, and cook until beans are tender-crisp (about 2 minutes); set aside.

Crumble beef into wok and stir-fry until no longer pink. Add onion and garlic and stir-fry until limp (about 3 minutes). Return beans to wok and add egg mixture, turning until eggs are set to your liking. Sprinkle nuts over top. Makes 4 servings.

Crab and Beef Stir-fry

It may never have occurred to you to combine crab with beef. But with the addition of a few vegetables, it is a delicious way of using up leftover roast beef or steak in a stir-fry dish.

    2 to 3 ounces dried Chinese noodles or fine
          spaghetti
       Boiling salted water
    2 tablespoons salad oil
    ¼ pound mushrooms, cut in ¼-inch slices
    1 teaspoon ground ginger
    2 cloves garlic, minced or pressed
    1 teaspoon grated lemon peel
    ½ pound crab meat or 1 can (7 oz.)
          crab meat
    1 can (4 or 6 oz.) water chestnuts, drained
          and thinly sliced
    ½ package (10 oz.) frozen peas, thawed
    1 to 1½ cups cooked lean beef (roast or
          steak), cut in matchstick-size pieces
    3 tablespoons soy sauce
    ½ pound bean sprouts
    3 eggs
    2 green onions, finely chopped

Cook noodles in boiling salted water for about 7 minutes or until barely tender; drain, rinse under cold water, drain again, and set aside.

Place wok over high heat. When wok is hot, add oil. When oil is hot, add mushrooms, ginger, garlic, and lemon peel. Stir-fry for about 2 minutes or until mushrooms are limp. Stir in crab, water chestnuts, peas, and beef. Stir-fry for about 2 minutes. Add 1 tablespoon of the soy; cover and simmer for about 1 minute. Stir in noodles and bean sprouts. Beat eggs with remaining 2 tablespoons soy. Pour over mixture and cook for about 1 minute, stirring to coat ingredients. Sprinkle with green onion. Makes 4 servings.

Beef Strips and Cherry Tomatoes

Serve this beef dish over crunchy canned chow mein noodles or use regular noodles for variation.

    1 pound boneless lean beef
          (sirloin or flank)
    2 tablespoons soy sauce
    1 teaspoon *each* sugar and minced fresh
          ginger root
    1 clove garlic, minced or pressed
       Cooking sauce (directions follow)
       About 5 tablespoons salad oil
    ¼ pound mushrooms, thinly sliced
    1 medium-size onion, cut in squares
    1 medium-size green pepper, seeded and
          cut in 1-inch squares
   1½ cups cherry tomatoes, halved

Cut beef with the grain into 1½-inch-wide strips. Cut each strip across the grain in ⅛-inch-thick slanting slices. Combine soy, sugar, ginger, garlic, and beef, mixing to coat meat well. Let stand for 15 minutes to marinate.

Prepare cooking sauce and set aside.

Place wok over high heat. When wok is hot, add 1 tablespoon of the oil. When oil is hot, add half the meat mixture and stir-fry until browned (about 2 minutes); remove meat from wok and set aside. Repeat, using 1 more tablespoon oil and remaining meat.

Heat remaining 3 tablespoons oil in wok. When oil is hot, add mushrooms and onion. Stir-fry for about 2 minutes. Add green pepper and stir-fry for about 1 minute. Return meat to pan, add tomatoes, and stir-fry to heat through (about 1 minute). Add cooking sauce and stir until it boils and thickens (about 1 minute). Makes 2 to 4 servings.

Cooking sauce. Mix together 1 tablespoon *each* **cornstarch** and **soy sauce**, 1 teaspoon **sugar**, and ½ cup **regular-strength beef broth**.

Oyster Beef

Rich, dark brown oyster sauce is the predominant flavoring that coats this thinly sliced beef. It is bottled and can usually be found in the Oriental section of your grocery store.

  1 **pound boneless lean beef (flank,**
       sirloin, or top round)
  2 **green onions, thinly sliced**
  2 **tablespoons** *each* **soy sauce and water**
  1 **tablespoon** *each* **cornstarch and**
       white wine or water
  ½ **teaspoon salt**
  2 **tablespoons** *each* **salad oil and oyster**
       sauce
  1 **teaspoon sugar**

Cut beef with the grain into 1½-inch-wide strips. Cut each strip across the grain in ⅛-inch-thick slanting slices. Combine onion, soy, water, cornstarch, wine, salt, and beef, mixing to coat meat well. Let stand for 15 minutes to marinate.

Place wok over high heat. When wok is hot, add 1 tablespoon of the oil. When oil is hot, add half the meat mixture and stir-fry until browned (about 2 minutes); remove from wok. Repeat, using remaining 1 tablespoon oil and meat mixture. Return cooked meat to wok. Add oyster

sauce and sugar and stir-fry for about 1 minute. Makes 3 or 4 servings.

Beef Stroganoff

The fragrance of grated nutmeg and the piquancy of Dijon mustard distinguishes this stroganoff from others. Serve over hot, cooked noodles.

  1½ **pounds boneless lean beef**
         Pepper
  5 **tablespoons butter or margarine**
  1 **medium-size onion, finely chopped**
  ½ **pound mushrooms, cut in ¼-inch-thick**
       slices
  3 **tablespoons all-purpose flour**
  1 **cup condensed beef bouillon**
  1 **tablespoon Dijon mustard**
  ¼ **teaspoon freshly grated nutmeg**
  ½ **cup whipping cream**
       Hot, cooked, buttered noodles
       Chopped parsley

Cut beef across the grain in ¼-inch-thick slanting slices. Sprinkle meat generously with pepper.

Place wok over medium-high heat. When wok is hot, add 1 tablespoon of the butter. When butter has melted, add onion and stir-fry until limp (about 2 minutes). Add half the meat and stir-fry until browned on all sides (about 5 minutes); remove from wok. Repeat, using 1 more tablespoon butter and remaining meat; remove from wok.

Add the remaining 3 tablespoons butter. When butter has melted, add mushrooms and stir-fry until limp (about 2 minutes). Add flour and stir-fry for about 30 seconds. Reduce heat to medium, add broth and mustard, and stir until thickened (about 1 minute). Return meat-onion mixture to pan, add nutmeg and cream, and stir until heated through. Serve over buttered noodles and garnish with parsley. Makes 4 to 6 servings.

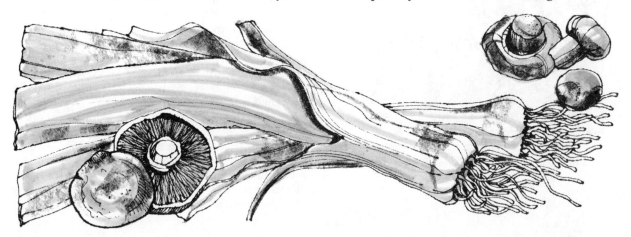

Steak and Asparagus

Round steak and flank steak are good cuts of meat for stir-frying. If you partially freeze the meat, it's easier to cut into thin slices.

1 to 1½ pounds boneless lean beef
2 tablespoons *each* soy sauce and dry sherry
⅛ teaspoon pepper
1 teaspoon sugar
  Cooking sauce (directions follow)
  About 4 tablespoons salad oil
1 large clove garlic, minced or pressed
1 teaspoon minced fresh ginger root or ½ teaspoon ground ginger
¾ pound cauliflower, cut into flowerets, then in ⅛-inch slices.
4 tablespoons water
1 pound asparagus (tough ends removed), cut in ½-inch-thick slanting slices
½ cup salted cashews or almonds, chopped

Cut beef with the grain into 1½-inch-wide strips. Cut each strip across the grain in ⅛-inch-thick slanting slices. Combine soy, sherry, pepper, sugar, and beef, mixing to coat meat well. Let stand for 15 minutes to marinate.

Meanwhile, prepare cooking sauce and set aside.

Place wok over high heat. When wok is hot, add 1 tablespoon of the oil. When oil is hot, add half the beef and stir-fry until browned (about 2 min-utes); remove meat from wok and keep warm. Repeat, using 1 more tablespoon oil and remaining meat.

Heat 1 more tablespoon oil in wok. When oil is hot, add garlic, ginger, and cauliflower. Stir-fry for 30 seconds. Add 3 tablespoons water; cover and cook, stirring frequently for about 3 minutes or until tender-crisp. Remove from wok and set aside. Add another tablespoon oil to wok. When oil is hot, add asparagus. Stir-fry for about 1 minute. Add remaining water, cover, and cook, stirring frequently, 2 minutes. Return cauliflower mixture to wok; add cooking sauce and stir until it boils and thickens (about 1 minute). Spoon over meat and sprinkle with nuts. Makes 4 servings.

Cooking sauce. Mix together 1½ tablespoons **cornstarch**, 1 teaspoon **sugar**, ½ teaspoon **salt**, and 1 cup **regular-strength chicken broth**.

Beef-Vegetable Stir-fry

Another inventive stir-fry combines lean beef, mushrooms, and edible-pod peas with traditional Oriental seasonings.

1 tablespoon cornstarch
1 teaspoon sugar
¼ teaspoon ground ginger
2 tablespoons soy sauce
½ cup regular-strength beef broth
1 pound boneless lean beef (flank or top round)
  About 5 tablespoons salad oil
1 clove garlic, minced or pressed
1 large onion, cut in half, then in ¼-inch slices
¼ pound mushrooms, sliced ¼ inch thick
¾ pound edible-pod peas, ends and strings removed

Mix together cornstarch, sugar, and ginger. Blend in soy and beef broth; set aside.

Cut beef with the grain into 1½-inch-wide strips. Cut each strip across the grain in ⅛-inch-thick slanting slices.

Place wok over high heat. When wok is hot, add 2 tablespoons of the oil. When oil is hot, add garlic and half the beef. Stir-fry until meat is lightly browned (about 2 minutes); remove from wok and set aside. Repeat, using 1 more tablespoon oil and remaining meat. Heat the remaining 2 table-spoons oil in wok, then add onion and mushrooms. Stir-fry for about 2 minutes. Add peas and stir-fry for about 1 minute. Return meat to pan, add corn-starch mixture, and stir until sauce boils and thickens (about 1 minute). Makes 4 servings.

Singing rice.... rehearse it first

Singing rice (or sizzling rice) adds the dimension of sound to dining. The golden crisp-fried rice sizzles and sings when hot soups or sauced foods are poured over it.

Although it is easy to prepare, you must start the singing rice at least a day ahead, and you must plan a menu that allows you to deep-fry the rice 5 minutes before serving the dish. Your guests have to be seated before you bring the piping hot rice to the table; then, when you pour the accompanying soup over it, they'll hear it sing.

Because rice, food, and containers must be hot, you may want to rehearse by positioning the accessories first.

Singing Fried Rice

A day or more in advance, combine 1 cup **long-grain rice,** 4 cups **water,** and 2 teaspoons **salt** in a 2-quart saucepan. Let stand ½ hour. Bring to a boil, cover, and simmer for 30 minutes. Drain; spread evenly on a heavily greased cooky sheet. Bake in a 250° oven for about 8 hours (occasionally open oven door and turn rice with a spatula).

Break the crusty rice into bite-size pieces. You can store rice in airtight containers or bags in your refrigerator for several weeks.

Just before serving time, heat oven to 250° and place in it a 1½-quart bowl or soup tureen to warm; also heat a soup bowl or pitcher in which to bring the accompanying soup to the table.

Place wok in ring stand. Add **salad oil** to a depth of about 2 inches and heat to 425° on a deep-fat-frying thermometer, add rice and cook, stirring, until golden brown (about 4 minutes); remove with a slotted spoon, drain, and transfer to warmed soup bowl. Bring to table and pour hot soup (directions follow) over rice.

Mushroom Singing Rice Soup

2 cans (about 13 oz. *each*) regular-strength chicken broth
⅓ pound lean pork, finely diced
1 clove garlic, minced or pressed
1 tablespoon soy sauce
¼ cup *each* sliced fresh mushrooms, sliced water chestnuts, and frozen green peas (thawed)
 Singing fried rice
 (see preceding directions)

Pour chicken broth into a 1½-quart saucepan; add pork, garlic, and soy; simmer for 10 minutes. Add mushrooms, water chestnuts, and peas. Cover and simmer for 2 minutes. Turn into a warm, heatproof pitcher or bowl and keep hot.

Fry crusty rice (as directed above) and turn half of it into preheated 1½-quart serving bowl or soup tureen. Carry soup and tureen of rice to table and quickly pour soup over hot rice. Serve remaining fried rice in a small bowl as an accompaniment to soup. Makes 4 to 6 servings.

Beef Teriyaki

You can use almost any lean boneless cut of beef, pork, or lamb in this dish. Cutting it in thin, slanting slices is part of the trick. It's easier to do if meat is partially frozen.

1 pound boneless lean beef
 Teriyaki marinade (directions follow)
 About 2 tablespoons salad oil
 Hot cooked rice (optional)
 Sliced green onion or chopped parsley
 (optional)

Cut beef across the grain in ⅛-inch-thick slanting slices. Prepare teriyaki marinade. Then add beef, mixing to coat meat well; let stand for 15 minutes to marinate, then drain.

Place wok over high heat. When wok is hot, add 1 tablespoon of the oil. When oil is hot, add half the meat mixture; stir-fry until browned (about 2 minutes). Remove to a bed of hot rice or warm serving platter. Repeat, using 1 more tablespoon oil and remaining meat. Garnish with onion, if you wish. Makes 3 or 4 servings.

Teriyaki marinade. Mix together 3 tablespoons **soy sauce,** 2 tablespoons *each* **sugar** and **dry sherry,** and ½ teaspoon minced fresh **ginger root.**

Stir-fried Sweet and Sour Pork

There are endless variations of sweet and sour pork; the one that follows is both quick and colorful—studded with green pepper, yellow pineapple, and red tomatoes.

> Sweet and sour sauce (directions follow)
> 2 **pounds boneless lean pork (such as butt or loin end), cut in 1-inch cubes**
> 1 **egg, beaten**
>   **About ½ cup cornstarch**
>   **About 5 tablespoons salad oil**
> 1 **medium-size onion, cut in 1-inch squares**
> 2 **medium-size carrots, cut in ¼-inch slanting slices**
> 1 **clove garlic, minced or pressed**
> 2 **tablespoons water**
> 1 **green pepper, seeded and cut in 1-inch squares**
> ½ **cup fresh pineapple chunks or canned pineapple chunks, drained**
> 2 **medium-size tomatoes, cut in 1-inch cubes**

Prepare sweet and sour sauce and set aside.

Dip pork pieces in beaten egg, drain briefly, and roll in cornstarch until lightly coated; shake off excess.

Place wok over medium-high heat. When wok is hot, add about 3 tablespoons of the oil. When oil is hot, add half the pork and stir-fry until browned (about 7 minutes); remove pork from wok and set aside. Repeat, adding more oil if necessary and remaining meat. Scrape away any browned particles and discard, but leave oil in pan. If necessary, add more oil to wok to make about 2 tablespoons total. Place wok over high heat. Add onion, carrot, and garlic; stir-fry for about 1 minute. Add water and green pepper; cover and cook, stirring frequently, for about 2 minutes. Add pineapple, tomato, pork, and sweet and sour sauce; stir until mixture boils and thickens (about 1 minute).

Sweet and sour sauce. Blend 1 tablespoon **cornstarch** with ⅓ cup firmly packed **brown sugar.** Stir in ½ teaspoon minced **fresh ginger root** (or ¼ teaspoon ground ginger), 1 tablespoon *each* **soy sauce** and **dry sherry,** and ¼ cup *each* **wine vinegar** and **regular-strength chicken broth** or beef broth.

Stir-fried Pork with Baby Corn

You may have noticed tiny ears of corn in gourmet sections of supermarkets or in Oriental food stores. Sold in cans or jars (don't use the pickled corn here), they're called baby or midget sweet corn. This is a special miniature variety, so tender that you can eat the cob, too.

> Cooking sauce (directions follow)
> 1 **pound boneless lean pork**
> 2 **cloves garlic, minced or pressed**
> ¼ **teaspoon pepper**
> 4 **tablespoons salad oil**
> 1 **small onion, cut in half, then in ¼-inch strips**
> ¼ **pound mushrooms, thinly sliced**
> 8 **green onions, cut in 2-inch lengths**
> 1 **can (about 1 lb.) whole baby sweet corn, drained**

Prepare cooking sauce and set aside.

Cut pork with the grain into 1½-inch-wide strips. Cut each strip across the grain in ⅛-inch-thick slanting slices. Mix garlic and pepper with pork strips; set aside.

Place wok over high heat. When wok is hot, add 1 tablespoon of the oil. When oil is hot, add half the pork mixture and stir-fry until pork is lightly browned (about 4 minutes); remove pork from wok and set aside. Repeat, using another 1 tablespoon oil and remaining meat.

Heat the remaining 2 tablespoons oil in wok. Add onion and mushrooms and stir-fry for about 1 minute. Add green onion and stir-fry for 30 seconds. Return pork to wok along with corn and cooking sauce and stir until pork is heated through and sauce thickens (about 1 minute). Makes 3 servings.

Cooking sauce. Mix together 1½ tablespoons **cornstarch**, 1 teaspoon *each* **sugar** and **vinegar**, ¼ teaspoon **salt**, 2 tablespoons **soy sauce**, and ¾ cup **regular-strength beef broth**.

Chinese Beef and Potatoes

Potatoes are not native to China but cooks there have adapted this western vegetable to their style of cooking. The potatoes quickly absorb the zesty flavor of ginger.

    Cooking sauce (directions follow)
1 tablespoon salad oil
1 large onion, thinly sliced
2 stalks celery, thinly sliced
1 pound lean ground beef
2 cloves garlic, minced or pressed
1½ teaspoons minced fresh ginger root or
    ¾ teaspoon ground ginger
2 medium-size new potatoes (about 1 lb.),
    peeled and cut in ½-inch cubes
2 cups water
1 beef bouillon cube
¼ cup soy sauce
1 jar (4 oz.) sliced pimentos, drained
    Salt
⅓ cup thinly sliced green onions

Prepare cooking sauce and set aside.
    Place wok over high heat. When wok is hot, add oil. When oil is hot, add onion and celery. Stir-fry for about 3 minutes or just until tender-crisp; set aside.
    Crumble beef into pan. Add garlic and ginger. Stir-fry until meat is browned (about 4 minutes). Skim off and discard any excess fat. Add potatoes, water, bouillon cube, and soy. Bring to a boil, cover, and simmer, stirring occasionally, until potatoes are tender when pierced (about 10 minutes).
    Add onion and celery mixture, pimento, and cooking sauce. Cook, stirring, until sauce boils and thickens (about 1 minute). Add salt to taste and garnish with green onion. Makes 3 or 4 servings.

Cooking sauce. Mix together 2 tablespoons *each* **cornstarch** and **water**, ¼ teaspoon **pepper**, and ½ teaspoon **sesame oil** (optional).

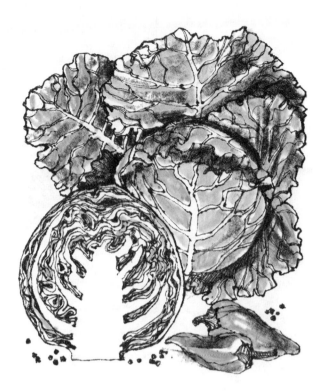

Chard and Sausage Scramble

Mild Italian sausage and Swiss chard are accented with garlic and topped with tomato wedges. Serve with French bread and butter. For a variation, try the dish with spinach instead of chard.

½ pound mild Italian sausage, casings
    removed
1 onion, finely chopped
1 clove garlic, minced or pressed
1 package (about 10 oz.) frozen chopped
    Swiss chard or chopped spinach,
    thawed and drained well
6 to 8 eggs, lightly beaten
    Tomato wedges
    Grated Parmesan cheese

Place wok over high heat. When wok is hot, crumble in sausage. Stir-fry until lightly browned (about 4 minutes). Discard all but 1 tablespoon drippings. Add onion and garlic and stir-fry until onion is limp (about 2 minutes). Add chard and stir-fry until all liquid has evaporated (about 1 minute).
    Reduce heat to medium. Pour eggs over chard and cook, gently lifting cooked portion from bottom to allow uncooked portion to flow underneath. Cook until set to your liking. Accompany with tomato wedges and grated Parmesan cheese to sprinkle over. Makes 4 to 6 servings.

Add oil to wok. When oil is hot, add mushrooms and zucchini and stir-fry for 30 seconds. Add hot water, sherry, and chicken stock base; cover and cook for 2 minutes. Return sausage and carrot mixture to wok and cook, uncovered, for 30 seconds or until most of liquid has evaporated. Serve with Parmesan cheese. Makes 4 servings.

Pork Tenderloin Apple Sauté

Pork tenderloin is cut in thin, slanting slices to sauté to succulency with apples and onions.

- ½ teaspoon *each* salt and oregano leaves
- ⅛ teaspoon pepper
- 3 tablespoons all-purpose flour
  About ¾ pound pork tenderloin, cut in ⅛-inch slanting slices
- 4 tablespoons butter or margarine
- 1 large onion, chopped
- 1 large Golden Delicious apple, cored and thinly sliced
- 2 tablespoons Dijon mustard
- 1 cup milk
- 2 tablespoons *each* sweet pickle relish and raisins
  Chopped parsley

Combine salt, oregano, pepper, and flour. Dredge meat in flour mixture; shake off excess. Set remaining flour mixture aside.

Place wok over medium-high heat. When wok is hot, add 2 tablespoons of the butter. When butter has melted, add pork and stir-fry until browned (about 4 minutes); remove pork from wok and set aside. Add the remaining 2 tablespoons butter and onion and stir-fry until onion is limp (about 2 minutes). Add remaining flour mixture and apple; stir-fry for about 1 minute. Add mustard and milk; bring to a boil, then return meat to wok and stir-fry for about 2 minutes. Stir in relish and raisins and sprinkle with parsley. Makes 3 or 4 servings.

Italian Sausage and Zucchini

Sausage encases convenient flavor for the cook who wants to turn out interesting, distinctive dishes in a hurry. Mild Italian sausage is combined here with zucchini and mushrooms. Use Italian hot sausage if you like.

  About 1 pound mild Italian sausage
- 1 medium-size onion, cut in half and thinly sliced
- 1 pound carrots, cut in ¼-inch slanting slices
- 1 tablespoon water
- 1 tablespoon salad oil
- ¼ pound mushrooms, cut in ¼-inch slices
- 1 pound zucchini, cut in ¼-inch slices
- ¼ cup *each* hot water and dry sherry
- 1 teaspoon chicken stock base or 1 chicken bouillon cube
  Grated Parmesan cheese

Remove casings from sausage and crumble meat. Place wok over high heat. When wok is hot, add sausage and stir-fry until browned (about 5 minutes); remove sausage from wok with a slotted spoon and set aside.

To drippings in wok, add onion and carrot. Stir-fry for about 1 minute. Add the 1 tablespoon water; cover and cook for 3 minutes or until carrot is tender-crisp; remove from wok and set aside.

Five-spice Pork and Potatoes

Fragrant Chinese five-spice is a typical Chinese seasoning that varies from chef to chef. It is absorbed by the potatoes in this dish. If you can't find it on the spice shelf in your market, use our equally delicious alternative. The dish is partially stir-fried, then simmered until tender.

3 medium-size baking potatoes
(about 1½ lbs.)
2 tablespoons salad oil
1 pound boneless lean pork (such as
shoulder or butt), cut into 1 by
3-inch strips
2 cloves garlic, minced or pressed
1½ cups water
3 tablespoons soy sauce
2 teaspoons sugar
1¼ teaspoons Chinese five-spice (or ½
teaspoon ground ginger, ¼ teaspoon
each ground cinnamon and crushed anise
seed, and ⅛ teaspoon *each* ground allspice and ground cloves)
⅓ cup thinly sliced green onion

Cut potatoes crosswise into ½-inch-thick slices; cut large slices in half. Place wok over high heat. When wok is hot, add oil. When oil is hot, add pork and garlic. Stir-fry until pork is browned (about 5 minutes). Add potatoes, water, soy, sugar, and Chinese five-spice. Bring to a boil, cover, and simmer, stirring occasionally, until potatoes are tender when pierced (about 20 minutes). Garnish with green onion. Makes 3 or 4 servings.

Chinese Almond Omelet

For an after-the-theater supper for eight, make this large open-faced omelet with cooked ham and canned mushrooms.

12 eggs
2 tablespoons instant minced onion
2 teaspoons soy sauce
¼ teaspoon minced fresh ginger root or
⅛ teaspoon ground ginger
2 tablespoons butter or margarine
1 can (6 oz.) sliced mushrooms, drained
1½ cups thinly sliced celery
¼ pound cooked ham, cut in thin strips
(about 1 cup)
⅓ cup slivered almonds
Soy sauce

Beat eggs with onion, the 2 teaspoons soy, and ginger; set aside.

Place wok over medium-high heat. When wok is hot, add butter. When butter has melted, add mushrooms, celery, and ham. Stir-fry until celery is limp (about 2 minutes).

Reduce heat to medium-low. Pour in egg mixture. Cook, gently lifting cooked portion with spatula to allow uncooked egg to flow underneath. When cooked to your liking, sprinkle with almonds. Pass additional soy to serve over. Makes 8 servings.

Fried Tofu with Pork Sauce

Here's a high-protein dish—you stir-fry together pork, vegetables, and deep-fried tofu puffs. For a description of tofu, see page 38.

Cooking sauce (directions follow)
2 tablespoons salad oil
2 cloves garlic, minced or pressed
¾ pound boneless lean pork, cut in
½ by 2-inch slices
2 stalks celery, thinly sliced
6 green onions, cut in 2-inch lengths
¼ pound small cooked shrimp
About 2 ounces Japanese-style deep-
fried tofu puffs, cut in 1-inch cubes,
or 5 ounces Chinese-style deep-fried
tofu puffs
Salt

Prepare cooking sauce and set aside.

Place wok over high heat. When wok is hot, add oil. When oil is hot, add garlic and pork. Stir-fry until meat is lightly browned (about 5 minutes). Add celery and stir-fry for about 1 minute. Stir in onion, shrimp, and cooking sauce. Cook, stirring, until sauce boils and thickens (about 1 minute). Add tofu and stir until heated through. Add salt to taste. Makes 3 or 4 servings.

Cooking sauce. Mix together 1 tablespoon **cornstarch**, ¼ teaspoon *each* **pepper** and **ground ginger**, 2 tablespoons *each* **soy sauce** and **dry sherry**, and ⅔ cup **regular-strength chicken broth**.

DEEP-FRYING IN A WOK

The secret of crispy-tender deep-fried
foods is to have the cooking oil very hot and keep it
that way. If it isn't hot enough for
the amount of food being cooked, foods soak up
too much oil and become greasy. To ensure
constant temperature while cooking,
use a deep-fat-frying thermometer or an electric wok
with its own heat control.

How to deep-fry in a wok

Anything that can be cooked in a deep-fryer can be done in a wok, usually with less oil. Unless yours is an electric or flat-bottomed wok, you'll need to use a ring stand to support and stabilize the wok over your burner or element and prevent it from tipping when it's filled with hot oil.

Place the wok over the heat source, pour in the oil, and bring it to the temperature required in the recipe you're using. Fry small amounts at a time—adding too much food at once lowers the temperature of the oil. Be careful when you add moist foods, for they tend to spatter.

It's handy to use a wire skimmer for straining off particles of food from the oil before they burn and for lifting out cooked foods; a slotted spoon will do, though. Also handy to have is a wire semicircular rack that can be attached to the top of the wok for draining cooked foods (see photograph on page 7).

Handle a wok full of hot oil very carefully, allowing the oil to cool before trying to pour it out. Then strain the oil and you can use it again.

Spinach and Mushroom Croquettes

Crispy crusts and hot creamy fillings—the contrasting textures of vegetable croquettes lend elegance to a plain meal.

The vegetables are bonded in a thick cream sauce, chilled, then coated with bread crumbs before frying. They can be shaped and fried ahead, then reheated.

- 6 tablespoons butter or margarine
- 1 small onion, chopped
- 1 clove garlic, minced or pressed
- ¼ pound mushrooms, chopped
- 4 tablespoons all-purpose flour, unsifted
- ¼ teaspoon salt
- ⅛ teaspoon ground nutmeg
- 1 cup milk
- 1 package (10 oz.) frozen chopped spinach, thawed
- ¼ cup grated Parmesan cheese
- 2 eggs, separated
- 2 tablespoons water
- 1½ cups fine dry bread crumbs
  Salad oil

Place wok over medium-high heat. Add 4 tablespoons of the butter. When butter has melted, add onion, garlic, and mushrooms. Stir-fry until vegetables are limp and all liquid has evaporated (about 3 minutes). Add remaining 2 tablespoons butter. When butter has melted, blend in flour, salt, and nutmeg. Remove wok from heat and gradually stir in milk. Return wok to medium-low heat and cook mixture, stirring, until thickened.

Squeeze out and discard all liquid from spinach. Stir into wok along with Parmesan cheese and the 2 egg yolks. Cook, stirring, just until mixture bubbles. Spread evenly into an ungreased 8 or 9-inch square baking pan. Cool, cover, and chill thoroughly (at least 3 hours or as long as overnight).

In a bowl, beat the 2 egg whites with water until blended. Place bread crumbs on a piece of wax paper. Divide cold vegetable mixture into 9 equal-size parts and, with floured hands, shape each portion into a ball. Dip each ball into egg white mixture, then roll in crumbs to coat completely. Cover and chill until firm (at least 2 hours or as long as overnight).

Place wok in ring stand. Pour oil into wok to a depth of about 1½ to 2 inches and heat to 375° on a deep-fat-frying thermometer. Fry 2 or 3 croquettes at a time, turning them occasionally, until browned (3 to 4 minutes). Remove with a slotted spoon and drain. Serve immediately, or place in a 350° oven to keep warm.

If made ahead, cool thoroughly, cover, and refrigerate for as long as 2 days. To reheat, place in a single layer on shallow baking sheet and bake, uncovered, in a 375° oven until hot and crisp (20 to 25 minutes). Makes 9 croquettes.

Curried Carrot Croquettes

Crumb-coated carrot croquettes are fried golden and crisp in hot oil. Inside their crispy crust are shredded carrots in a creamy curry sauce. They make a delicious accompaniment to pork chops.

- 6 tablespoons butter or margarine
- 1 small onion, chopped
- 1 clove garlic, minced or pressed
- 2 cups shredded carrot
- ½ teaspoon *each* curry powder and salt
- ¼ teaspoon ground coriander
  Dash cayenne
- 4½ tablespoons all-purpose flour, unsifted
- 1 cup milk
- 2 tablespoons chopped parsley
- 2 eggs, separated
- 2 tablespoons water
- 1½ cups fine dry bread crumbs
  Salad oil

(Continued on next page)

Place wok over medium-high heat. Add 4 table-spoons of the butter. When butter has melted, add onion, garlic, carrot, curry powder, salt, coriander, and cayenne. Stir-fry until vegetables are limp (about 3 minutes). Add remaining 2 tablespoons butter. When butter has melted, blend in flour. Remove wok from heat and gradually stir in milk and parsley. Return wok to medium-low heat and cook mixture, stirring, until thickened. Add the 2 egg yolks and cook, stirring, just until mixture bubbles. Spread evenly into an ungreased 8 or 9-inch square baking pan, then cool, cover, and chill thoroughly (at least 3 hours or as long as overnight).

In a bowl, beat the 2 egg whites with water until blended. Place bread crumbs on a piece of wax paper. Divide cold vegetable mixture into 9 equal-size parts and, with floured hands, shape each portion into a ball. Dip each ball into egg white mixture, then roll in crumbs to coat completely. Cover and chill until firm (at least 2 hours or as long as overnight).

Place wok in ring stand. Pour oil into wok to a depth of about 1½ to 2 inches and heat to 375° on a deep-fat-frying thermometer. Fry 2 or 3 croquettes at a time, turning them occasionally, until browned (3 to 4 minutes). Remove with a slotted spoon and drain on paper towels. Serve immediately, or place in a 350° oven to keep warm.

If made ahead, cool thoroughly, cover, and refrigerate for as long as 2 days. To reheat, place in a single layer on a shallow baking sheet and bake, uncovered, in a 375° oven until hot and crisp (20 to 25 minutes). Makes 9 croquettes.

Chicken and Vegetable Fritters

Dip bite-size chunks of chicken and vegetables into flour and egg to make these simple fritters; or, if you like, dice the vegetables, mix with egg and milk, then form into small patties to fry golden brown. Serve with a smooth shrimp bisque and a tossed green salad for dinner.

    4 or 5 cups vegetables (eggplant,
        cauliflower, and squash)
    3 whole chicken breasts (about 1 lb. *each*),
        skinned, boned, and cut into bite-
        size pieces
      All-purpose flour
      Salt
    8 eggs, beaten
      Salad oil
      Sauce rosa (directions follow)

Cut eggplant into ½ by 2-inch pieces; break cauli-flower into small flowerets; cut squash (zucchini, patty pan, or crookneck) into 1-inch-thick pieces or sticks. Dust vegetables and chicken chunks with flour; shake off excess. Then sprinkle with salt and dip into beaten egg.

Place wok in ring stand. Pour oil into wok to a depth of about 1½ inches and heat to 370° on a deep-fat-frying thermometer. Add chicken, cook, turning occasionally, until golden brown (about 3 minutes). Drain on paper towels. (This much can be done ahead. Place pieces in single layer on trays lined with paper towels and let stand for as long as 3 hours at room temperature. To reheat, remove paper towels and place in a 375° oven for about 10 minutes.) Serve with sauce rosa. Makes 6 to 8 servings.

For vegetable fritter patties, cut vegetables into ¼-inch dice. For each ¾ cup diced vegetables, blend 1 **egg**, 1 tablespoon **milk**, ¼ teaspoon **salt**, and 2 tablespoons **all-purpose flour**. Drop by spoonfuls into hot oil as directed above for pieces.

Sauce rosa. Blend together 1 cup **sour cream**, 2 tablespoons **tomato paste**, ½ teaspoon **paprika**, ¼ teaspoon **chile powder**, 2 teaspoons **brown sugar**, and 1 teaspoon **lemon juice**.

Spicy Chicken Tacos

Pictured on facing page

The mild flavor of chicken combines well with the sweetness of raisins and spiciness of chiles in these special chicken tacos. You can use leftover chicken or turkey or pork as the filling. For ease in shaping tacos, use a special rack or fold with tongs.

    1 tablespoon salad oil
    1 medium-size onion, finely chopped
    2 cups finely diced or shredded cooked
        chicken, turkey, or pork
    ¼ cup raisins
    1½ tablespoons sliced ripe olives
    ⅔ cup canned enchilada sauce or
        taco sauce
      Salad oil
    1 dozen corn tortillas
      Garnishes: tomato chunks, avocado
        slices, coriander leaves (Chinese
        parsley), shredded Cheddar cheese,
        chopped green onions, and
        lime wedges

Place wok over medium-high heat. When wok is hot, add the 1 tablespoon oil. When oil is hot, add onion and stir-fry until limp (about 2 minutes).

(Continued on page 52)

Tacos in a wok? Why not? Fry tortillas, fold,
drain on a rack or paper towels; then add
chicken-raisin-olive filling. The recipe is on page 50.

Reduce heat to medium and add chicken, raisins, olives, and enchilada sauce. Remove from wok and keep warm.

Rinse out wok and dry.

Place wok in ring stand. Pour in oil to a depth of about ½ inch, and heat to 375° on a deep-fat-frying thermometer. With tongs, slip one tortilla at a time into hot oil, folding in half when they become soft (just a few seconds) so there is a space between the halves for filling to be added later. Fry tortilla until crisp and light brown, turning as necessary to cook all sides (takes about 2 minutes).

To drain the half-moon shape taco shells, place in a taco rack (see page 51) or place on paper towels.

Spoon 3 to 4 tablespoons filling into each taco. Garnish with tomato chunks, avocado slices, cilantro leaves, shredded cheese, green onions, and lime wedges. Makes 12 tacos.

Mexican Chimichangas

Like burritos, chimechangas are made by wrapping flour tortillas around a spicy meat or bean filling. But, unlike burritos, they are fried until golden brown and crisp. Choose from two fillings: beef and bean or spicy pork. Fillings can be made ahead and frozen; or fully prepared chimechangas can be frozen, then reheated when needed.

>   Beef and bean filling (directions follow)
>   or Spicy pork filling (directions follow)
> 1   dozen flour tortillas
>   Salad oil
>   About 1½ cups homemade guacamole or
>   1 can (6 oz.) frozen guacamole, thawed
>   Tomato and green chile relish
>   (directions follow)
>   About 1½ cups sour cream

Prepare filling of your choice. Place ¼ cup of the mixture near center of each tortilla. Fold tortilla around filling, tucking in sides; fasten with wooden picks. (If tortillas are too brittle to roll, lightly dampen with water, wrap in foil, and heat in a 350° oven until warm and pliable.)

Place wok in ring stand. Pour oil into wok to a depth of about 1½ inches and heat to 370° on a deep-fat-frying thermometer. Add 3 or 4 chimechangas at a time and cook, turning as needed, until browned (about 5 minutes). Remove with tongs and drain on paper towels; keep warm.

If made ahead, cool thoroughly, cover, and refrigerate. For longer storage, wrap airtight and freeze. To reheat, place frozen chimechangas in a single layer in a shallow rimmed pan; bake, un-covered, in a 350° oven for about 25 minutes or until thoroughly heated.

Pass guacamole, tomato and green chile relish, and sour cream to spoon over. Makes 1 dozen or 4 to 6 servings.

Beef and bean filling. Place wok over medium-high heat. When wok is hot, add 1 tablespoon **salad oil**. When oil is hot, add ¾ pound lean **ground beef**, 1 large **onion** (chopped), 1 large **green pepper** (seeded and chopped), and 1 clove **garlic** (minced or pressed). Stir-fry until meat is lightly browned and onion is limp (about 3 minutes). Discard excess drippings. Stir in ½ teaspoon *each* **salt** and **ground cumin**, 2 tablespoons **chile powder**, ⅛ teaspoon **cayenne**, and ½ cup canned **refried beans**. Reduce heat to medium-low and cook, stirring, until heated through. Fold in 1 cup (about 4 oz.) shredded **jack cheese.**

Spicy pork filling. Cut 1 pound lean, **boneless pork** into ½-inch cubes. Place wok over high heat. When wok is hot, add 2 tablespoons **salad oil.** When oil is hot, add pork and stir-fry until lightly browned (about 2 minutes). Add 2 medium-size **onions** (chopped), 2 cloves **garlic** (minced or pressed), and 1 large **green pepper** (seeded and chopped); cook until onion is limp. Add ½ teaspoon *each* **salt** and **oregano leaves**, ¼ cup chopped fresh **coriander** (cilantro) or 1 tablespoon dry cilantro leaves, 1 can (4 oz.) diced **California green chiles**, and 2 tablespoons **water**. Cover and cook over low heat, stirring occasionally, for 35 minutes or until pork is fork-tender and liquid evaporates.

Tomato and green chile relish. Combine 1 pound (about 4 medium-size) **tomatoes**, peeled and diced, 1 can (4 oz.) diced **California green chiles**, ½ cup chopped **onion**, 1 tablespoon **vinegar**, 1 teaspoon **sugar**, ½ teaspoon **salt**, and ¼ teaspoon **pepper.**

Picnic Chicken Legs

There's no coating necessary for this variation of fried chicken, so they don't get soggy when taken along on a picnic. The chicken legs marinate in soy sauce for an hour, then are crisply fried in hot oil. Serve with potato salad and brownies.

   2 or 3 tablespoons soy sauce
   1 teaspoon pepper
   ½ teaspoon salt
   1 tablespoon sugar
  14 to 16 chicken drumsticks or 7 to 8 legs
        and thighs, separated (about 3 lbs.)
        Salad oil

Combine soy, pepper, salt, and sugar. Rub over chicken pieces to coat thoroughly. Let stand for 1 to 2 hours (or until next day) to marinate.

Place wok in ring stand. Pour oil into wok to a depth of about 1½ inches and heat to 375° on a deep-fat-frying thermometer. Drain off excess marinade from chicken and pat dry. Carefully add half of the chicken, one piece at a time, to hot oil; cook, turning frequently, for about 10 minutes or until meat is no longer pink near bone (cut a small gash to test). Drain on paper towels and keep warm while you repeat cooking procedure for remaining pieces. Makes 4 servings.

Chicken Wing Appetizers

Chicken wings look like tiny tom-tom drumsticks when they are pared down to provide their own little holders. You cut off the meatiest sections of the chicken wings and fry them crisp to dip into spicy barbecue sauce.

  24 chicken wings (about 4 to 5 lbs.)
        Salt and pepper
        Cornstarch
        Salad oil
        Bottled spicy barbecue sauce

Cut off the meatiest portion of each chicken wing at the first joint; reserve center section and tip for stock. Holding the small end of each large piece, trim around bone with a sharp knife to cut meat free. Then cut and scrape with knife to push meat down to large end of bone. Finally, with your fingers, pull portion of meat and skin down over end of bone. At this point you can cover and refrigerate for as long as overnight.

Just before frying, sprinkle wings lightly with salt and pepper then dust with cornstarch, shaking off excess.

Place wok in ring stand. Pour in oil to depth of 1½ inches and heat to 350° on a deep-fat-frying thermometer. Add 4 or 5 wings at a time and cook for 5 or 6 minutes or until golden brown, turning several times. Remove from oil with slotted spoon and drain on paper towels; keep warm in a 150° oven until all are cooked or for as long as 1 hour. Serve with barbecue sauce to dip. Makes 24 appetizers.

Short-cut doughnuts

Pictured on page 54

No need to make doughnuts from scratch. Try a shortcut—use frozen bread dough. You can cut the doughnuts into any size or shape you wish, from logs to knots to doughnut holes. Fry them; then sprinkle the still hot doughnuts with sugar or cinnamon and sugar.

   1 loaf (1 lb.) frozen bread dough
        All-purpose flour
        Salad oil
        Sugar or cinnamon and sugar

At room temperature, thaw bread dough as package directs, until dough is pliable (1 to 2 hours).

Cut thawed loaf crosswise and lengthwise to make 15 equal-size pieces (8 pieces for larger doughnuts). On a lightly floured board, roll into balls or shapes of your choice. For regular doughnuts, flatten and cut out holes. Place on greased cooky sheets and let rise in a warm place until very light and puffy (about 30 minutes).

Place wok in ring stand. Pour oil into wok to a depth of about 1½ inches and heat to 350° on a deep-fat-frying thermometer. Add 2 or 3 doughnuts at a time and fry, turning as needed, until golden brown on all sides (about 1½ minutes). Remove and drain on paper toweling. Coat doughnuts in sugar or cinnamon and sugar while hot. Makes 8 large or 16 small doughnuts.

*These easy doughnuts, made from refrigerator bread dough,
deep-fry crisp on the outside and cake-tender inside.
The recipe is on page 53.*

Falafil

Falafil are fried morsels made from highly seasoned legume flour (fava bean, garbanzo) that is laced with crunchy sesame seed. Originating in the Mediterranean countries, the flour is available here as a dry mix. You simply add water, shape into small balls, and fry in hot oil. For appetizers, dip into yogurt sauce (see below); for a sandwich, stuff into pocket (peda) bread with romaine lettuce.

  1 **cup dry falafil mix**
  ½ **cup water**
     Salad oil
     Yogurt sauce (directions follow)

Combine falafil mix and water; stir thoroughly until water is well absorbed, then shape into ¾-inch diameter balls.

    Place wok in ring stand. Pour oil into wok to a depth of about 1 inch and heat to 350° on a deep-fat-frying thermometer. Add falafil balls (do not crowd) and fry, turning occasionally, until richly browned (about 2½ minutes); drain on paper towels. Serve plain or with yogurt sauce. Makes 40 falafil; allow 3 to 4 per serving.

Yogurt sauce. Combine ½ cup **unflavored yogurt** with 1½ tablespoons *each* minced **green onion** and **chopped peeled cucumber**.

Spring Rolls

Ready-to-fill wrappers make the Chinese fried pastry, known as spring roll or egg roll, easy to duplicate at home. Serve them for appetizers or as part of a Chinese meal.

    The wrapper skins—similar to won ton skins, but larger—are available in Chinese markets or in the Oriental food sections of supermarket freezer areas. They are usually sold in 1 pound packages with about 2 dozen to a package.

     Ham filling (directions follow)
     Beef filling (directions follow)
     Sweet and sour sauce (directions follow)
  1 **package (1 lb.) spring roll or**
      egg roll skins
  1 **egg, beaten**
     Salad oil
     Soy sauce (optional)

Prepare ham or beef filling and cool. Prepare sweet and sour sauce and cool. Loosely wrap spring

roll skins in a damp towel to keep pliable. Mound about 2 rounded tablespoons cooled filling across each spring roll skin (be sure corner points toward you) in a 3½-inch log, about 2 inches above lower corner. Fold this corner over filling to cover, then roll over once to enclose filling. Dot left and right corners of triangle with beaten egg; fold corners over filling, pressing firmly to seal. Moisten remaining corner of skin with egg, then roll, sealing corner. Cover filled rolls with clear plastic wrap until ready to cook. (At this point, you can refrigerate up to 12 hours or wrap airtight and freeze.)

    Place wok in ring stand. Pour oil into wok to a depth of about 1½ inches and heat to 370° on a deep-fat-frying thermometer. Fry 4 or 5 rolls at a time, turning as needed, until golden brown (about 4 minutes). Remove with a slotted spoon and drain on paper towels.

    Cut rolls into thirds. Serve with sweet and sour sauce or soy sauce, if desired.

    (If made ahead, cool thoroughly, wrap airtight, and freeze. To reheat, place frozen rolls in a single layer in a shallow rimmed pan; bake, uncovered, for 25 minutes or until hot.) Makes about 2 dozen.

Ham filling. Prepare the following: 1 clove **garlic** (minced or pressed), ½ teaspoon grated **fresh ginger root**, 1 large **onion** (chopped), 1 cup thinly sliced **celery**; 1 pound **cooked ham** (cut into matchstick-size pieces), 1 can (6 oz.) drained **bamboo shoots** (cut into matchstick-size pieces), and 2 cups finely shredded **cabbage**.

    Combine 1 tablespoon **cornstarch**, ½ teaspoon **salt**, 2 teaspoons **soy sauce**, and 1 tablespoon **dry sherry**; set aside.

(Continued on next page)

Place wok over medium-high heat. When wok is hot, add 2 tablespoons **salad oil.** When oil is hot, add the garlic, ginger, onion, and celery. Stir-fry for about 1 minute.

Add ham, bamboo shoots, and cabbage; stir-fry for about 2 minutes. Stir in soy mixture, bring to a boil, and cook until thickened (about 30 seconds). Cool.

Beef filling. Prepare the following: 1 large **onion** (chopped), 2 cloves **garlic** (minced or pressed), and 1 pound *each* **zucchini** and **cabbage** (shredded); drain well, squeezing out all excess moisture.

Combine 1 tablespoon *each* **cornstarch** and **soy sauce,** 1½ teaspoons *each* **sugar** and **salt,** and ½ teaspoon **pepper;** set aside.

Place wok over high heat. When wok is hot, add 1 pound **lean ground beef,** stirring to break up meat, and cook until lightly browned. Drain all but 1 tablespoon drippings. Add onion and garlic; stir-fry for about 1 minute. Add zucchini and cabbage; stir-fry for about 2 minutes. Stir in soy mixture, bring to a boil, and cook until thickened (about 30 seconds). Cool.

Sweet and sour sauce. In a pan, combine 1½ teaspoons **cornstarch,** 3 tablespoons *each* **sugar** and **wine vinegar,** 1 tablespoon *each* **soy sauce** and tomato-based **chile sauce,** dash of **cayenne,** and ½ cup **regular-strength chicken broth.** Cook, stirring, until thickened.

Fried Won Ton

Pictured on page 48

These crisp-fried, triangular Chinese appetizers are made from a special won ton dough. It comes in skins in 1-pound packages that can be found in the produce section of markets.

Won tons are filled with savory pork, shrimp, or chorizo and beef fillings. Then they are deep-fried until crisp. A variety of sauces are usually provided for dipping.

> **Shrimp filling (directions follow)**
> **Pork filling (directions follow)**
> **Chorizo sausage and beef filling**
>   **(directions follow)**
> 1 package (1 lb.) won ton skins, thawed
>   if frozen
> 1 egg, beaten
>   Salad oil
>   Sauces for dipping (suggestions are
>   included in each filling recipe)

Prepare filling of your choice and cool.

To wrap, follow the illustration at right. 1. Hold won ton skin flat in your hand (cover remaining won ton skins with a damp towel to keep them pliable). Mound 1 teaspoon filling in corner near palm of hand. Dot that corner with beaten egg. 2. Fold that corner over filling, rolling to tuck point under. 3. Turn won ton 180°; moisten both corners at filling ends with egg. 4. Bring corners together, overlapping slightly. Pinch together firmly to seal. Repeat until all won ton skins are filled.

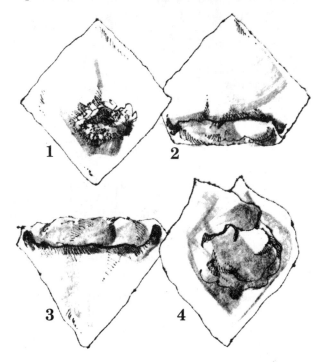

Place won tons side by side on a tray and cover with clear plastic wrap. (At this point, you can refrigerate up to 8 hours or wrap airtight and freeze.)

Place wok in ring stand. Pour oil into wok to a depth of about 2 inches and heat to 360° on a deep-fat-frying thermometer. Fry 4 to 6 prepared won tons at a time, turning occasionally, for 1 minute or until golden. Remove with a slotted spoon and drain on paper towels. Keep warm in a 200° oven until all are cooked, then serve.

If made ahead, cool thoroughly, wrap airtight, and refrigerate. Freeze for longer storage. To reheat, place in a single layer on shallow baking sheet and bake, uncovered, in a 350° oven for about 15 minutes or until crisp and hot throughout. Makes 5 to 7 dozen won ton.

Shrimp filling. Finely chop 1 pound shelled and deveined large raw **shrimp.** Stir in 1 can (4 to 6 oz.) **water chestnuts,** drained and chopped; 2 **green onions,** thinly sliced; 2 tablespoons **soy sauce;** and ⅛ teaspoon **garlic salt** until well blended. Wrap and fry as directed above. Serve with **chile sauce** or tartar sauce for dipping. Fills 5 to 6 dozen won ton skins.

Pork filling. Finely chop 1 can (4 to 6 oz.) drained **water chestnuts;** thinly slice 2 **green onions.** Stir together 1 tablespoon **dry sherry** and 1 teaspoon **cornstarch;** set aside.

Place wok over high heat. When wok is hot, crumble in 1 pound **lean ground pork** and stir-fry until brown (about 4 minutes); remove and discard excess drippings. Stir in chopped water chestnuts, green onion, 2 tablespoons **soy sauce,** ¼ teaspoon **garlic salt,** and the sherry-cornstarch mixture. Cook, stirring until thickened (about 1 minute). Cool, then wrap and fry as directed on page 56. Serve with **hot mustard** and **catsup** (separately) for dipping. Fills 6 to 7 dozen won ton skins.

Chorizo sausage and beef filling. Remove casings from 2 **chorizo sausages** (about 6 oz.). Thinly slice 1 **green onion.** Chop 2 canned **California green chiles.** Shred ½ cup **jack cheese.**

Place wok over medium-high heat. When wok is hot, crumble in chorizo sausage and ½ pound **lean ground beef.** Stir-fry for about 4 minutes or until browned. Discard excess drippings. Stir in green onion, green chile, and cheese. Cook, stirring, until cheese melts. Cool, then wrap and fry as directed on page 56. Serve with **guacamole** or frozen avocado dip (thawed). Fills 5 to 6 dozen won ton skins.

English Fish and Chips

An old English favorite, fish and chips is best when served piping hot. Deep-fry the French fries first and keep them warm while cooking the fish. If you want to be authentic, serve with malt vinegar as well as lemon wedges and salt.

 2 to 2½ pounds of mild, firm, white-fleshed
   fish fillets, *each* ½ to ¾ inch thick
 1 cup all-purpose flour, unsifted
 ½ teaspoon paprika
 ¼ teaspoon salt
 ⅛ teaspoon pepper
 ¾ cup beer
   Salad oil
 1½ pounds homemade (page 60) or frozen
   French-fried potatoes
   Malt vinegar (optional)
   Salt
   Lemon wedges

Cut fillets into 3 by 5-inch chunks; set aside.

Combine flour, paprika, salt, pepper, and beer, and beat until smooth; set aside.

Place wok in ring stand. Pour oil into wok to a depth of about 1½ to 2 inches and heat to 375° on a deep-fat-frying thermometer. Fry potatoes (according to directions on page 60, or as directed on package); drain and place in a warm oven.

Dip each piece of fish into beer batter, drain briefly, then place in hot oil. Fry a few pieces at a time, turning occasionally until golden brown (3 to 4 minutes). Remove with a slotted spoon, drain briefly, and place in oven with potatoes until all pieces are cooked.

Serve with malt vinegar, salt, and lemon wedges to sprinkle onto each portion. Serves 4.

Trout on Spinach Bed

Trout, pork, and spinach make an unusual but savory combination in this dish for two. The fried trout is presented on a bed of cooked spinach, then a pork and mushroom sauce is spooned over.

 6 medium-size Oriental dried mushrooms
   Hot water
 1 tablespoon cornstarch
 ¼ teaspoon salt
 ⅛ teaspoon pepper
 1 tablespoon *each* soy sauce and
   dry sherry
 ¾ cup regular-strength chicken broth
 2 trout (about ½ lb. *each*)
   Salt
   Cornstarch
   Salad oil
 1 bunch (about 1 lb.) spinach, washed
   and stems removed
 2 cloves garlic, minced or pressed
 ½ pound lean boneless pork, cut in
   1 by 2-inch strips
 1 teaspoon grated fresh ginger root
 2 green onions, thinly sliced

Rinse mushrooms, place in hot water to cover, and soak until soft and pliable (about 20 minutes). Trim off stems and discard, then cut mushrooms in thin strips.

Meanwhile, stir together the 1 tablespoon cornstarch, the ¼ teaspoon salt, pepper, soy, sherry, and chicken broth; set aside.

Rinse trout and pat dry. Sprinkle lightly with salt and coat each fish with cornstarch; shake off excess.

(Continued on next page)

Place wok in ring stand. Pour oil into wok to a depth of about 1 inch and heat to 400° on a deep-fat-frying thermometer. Add fish and cook until fish is crisp and browned (about 2½ minutes on a side). Drain on paper towels and keep warm.

Remove oil from wok and wipe any remaining bits of browned fish from wok. Place wok over high heat. When wok is hot, add 1 tablespoon oil. When oil is hot, add spinach and half the garlic. Stir-fry just until spinach wilts (about 30 seconds). Turn into a shallow serving dish.

Add 2 more tablespoons oil. When oil is hot, add remaining garlic, pork, and ginger. Stir-fry until pork is lightly browned (about 4 minutes). Add mushrooms and broth mixture; cook, stirring, until it boils and thickens (about 1 minute).

Arrange fish on spinach. Pour pork sauce over fish and sprinkle with sliced green onion. Makes 2 servings.

Tempura

Pictured on facing page

One of the most exquisite of deep-fried, batter-coated foods is Japanese tempura. The frittered seafood and vegetables are valued for their light, crisp coating.

The secret to tempura lies in using a cold, thin batter, lumpy with flour; the lumps help give tempura its lacy appearance.

Because you must make the batter and do the cooking just before serving, a tempura dinner is easier to prepare for just three or four guests. You might seat them at a counter or table near where you are cooking so you can serve the food quickly.

Cook several pieces at once, giving one or two pieces at a time to each guest. Serve immediately; the fragile crisp coating softens when it stands.

You might offer a clear soup for your guests to sip while you start the tempura frying. With the tempura serve pickled vegetables or sliced marinated cucumbers, as well as hot cooked rice. Prepare and set these at the table before beginning the tempura. The seafood and vegetables can be washed, dried, and chilled several hours ahead. Also make the dipping sauce in advance. Make the batter while the cooking oil heats.

> **Seafood** (suggestions follow)
> **Vegetables** (suggestions follow)
> **Tempura dipping sauce**
>   (directions follow)
> **About 1½ to 2 quarts salad oil**
> **Tempura batter** (directions follow)

Prepare seafood and vegetables as directed, and arrange on platters. Make the dipping sauce and pour it into individual serving bowls. Place wok in ring stand. Pour oil into wok to a depth of about 1½ to 2 inches and heat to 375° on a deep-fat-frying thermometer.

While oil heats, prepare tempura batter.

To cook tempura, dip prepared seafood and vegetables individually into batter with chopsticks or tongs. Let excess batter drip off, then gently lower pieces into hot oil. Cook several pieces at a time without crowding; turn occasionally until crisp and lightly golden (about 2 to 3 minutes). Remove with a slotted spoon and drain briefly on a wire rack set on a shallow pan. Serve immediately. As you continue frying, frequently skim off and discard any bits of batter remaining in oil.

To eat, dip each piece into tempura dipping sauce. Makes 4 servings.

Seafood. You'll need about 1 pound shrimp or fish (or a combination of the two). Use large, raw shrimp; remove shells except from around tail. Split shrimp along the back vein, cutting almost through the shrimp to make it lie flat; remove the vein. Rinse and pat dry.

For the fish, choose salmon, sole, or lingcod steaks or fillets. Cut away any bone or skin, then cut into 1½ by 3-inch strips about ¼-inch thick.

Vegetables. Choose 3 to 4 kinds from this list: 2 medium-size carrots, cut in 4-inch lengths, then in ¼-inch-thick lengthwise slices; ⅓ pound eggplant, cut in a thick wedge, then in ¼-inch-thick slices (to make eggplant fans as shown in photograph on page 59, cut ¼-inch-thick by 1-inch slices from top to bottom on diagonal, cutting almost all the way through); 1 dozen large mushrooms, cut in halves through stems; 1 medium-size sweet potato, peeled and cut in ¼-inch-thick rounds; 1 medium-size zucchini, cut in ¼-inch-thick diagonal slices.

Tempura dipping sauce. In a saucepan, combine 1 bottle (8 oz.) **clam juice** with ¼ cup *each* **soy sauce** and **dry sherry**. Bring to a boil, remove from heat, and let cool to room temperature. Finely shred enough **fresh ginger root** and **daikon** (white radish) to make 3 tablespoons *each;* pass ginger and daikon for guests to add to individual bowls of sauce according to taste.

Tempura batter. In a small bowl, lightly beat together 1 cup **ice cold water**, 1 **egg**, and ¼ teaspoon *each* **soda** and **salt**. Add 1 cup unsifted **cake flour**; mix just until blended (batter will be lumpy). Sprinkle another ⅓ cup unsifted **cake flour** over top of batter. With a fork, stir batter one or two strokes (do not blend thoroughly); most of the last addition of flour should be floating on top of the batter. Fill a larger bowl half full of ice; set the batter bowl in it to keep cold while you cook.

Lacy tempura batter coats deep-fried shrimp and vegetables.
The secret of light batter is cake flour.
The recipe is on page 58.

French Fried Shrimp and Onion Rings

Butterflied shrimp in a thin crisp coating is a perfect accompaniment for golden fried onion rings. Often featured in restaurants, they can be easily prepared at home. The onions, first soaked in milk, are sweet and mild and equally crisp.

> 1 large onion, sliced ¼ inch thick and separated into rings
> 1½ cups milk
> 2 pounds medium-size raw shrimp, shelled
> Salt
> All-purpose flour, unsifted
> 1 egg
> Salad oil

Combine onion rings and milk; let stand for 1 to 2 hours. Drain onions, reserving milk.

Split shrimp along back vein, cutting almost through the shrimp to make it lie flat; remove the vein. Rinse shrimp and pat dry, then sprinkle with about ¼ teaspoon salt and about 2 tablespoons flour, shaking off excess; set aside.

In a blender container, combine egg and 1 cup of the reserved milk. Add 1 cup flour and ½ teaspoon salt. Whirl until smooth.

Place wok in ring stand. Pour oil into wok to a depth of about 1½ inches and heat to 350° on a deep-fat-frying thermometer. Dip shrimp into batter; drain and place into oil (do not crowd). Cook until crisp and browned (about 2 minutes). Remove with a slotted spoon and drain on paper towels; keep warm.

Coat onion rings with batter and fry until crisp and browned (about 1 minute); drain on paper towels, sprinkle with salt, and serve with shrimp. Makes 4 servings.

French Fries

Traditional French fries in America are finger-size lengths of freshly cut potatoes fried quickly and salted lightly to be smothered in catsup by kids of all ages.

> 4 medium-size potatoes
> Water
> Salad oil
> Salt

Cut potatoes into finger-size sticks (about ½ inch by 3 inches). Soak in cold water up to ½ hour, changing water once. Drain and pat dry.

Place wok in ring stand. Pour oil into wok to a depth of about 1½ inches and heat to 375° on a deep-fat-frying thermometer. Fry about 10 sticks at a time, turning as needed, to brown all sides (3 to 4 minutes). Remove with a slotted spoon, drain on paper towels, and sprinkle with salt. Makes 4 servings.

Fish-stuffed Tofu

One way to prepare tofu (see page 38) is to stuff it with a savory fish mixture and fry it. In this version, tofu triangles are filled with a minced fish and onion mixture, fried, then simmered in a lightly seasoned sauce laced with lettuce and mushrooms. Serve it with hot cooked rice.

> 1 package (about 1 lb. 6 oz.) firm tofu squares
> Fish stuffing (directions follow)
> Salad oil
> 3 cloves garlic, minced or pressed
> 3 large iceberg lettuce leaves, cut in 2-inch squares (about 3 cups)
> ¼ cup frozen peas, thawed
> 1 can (4 oz.) whole mushrooms, drained
> 1 cup regular-strength chicken broth
> 2½ teaspoons cornstarch
> 2 tablespoons soy sauce or oyster sauce
> 1 tablespoon water

Cut tofu squares in half diagonally to make 8 triangles. Let drain in a colander for at least 15 minutes, then place between paper towels and gently press out excess water. On widest side of each triangle, cut a pocket to within ½-inch of edges. Gently fill each pocket with about 1½ teaspoons fish stuffing.

Place wok in ring stand. Pour oil into wok to a depth of about 1½ inches and heat to 350° on a deep-fat-frying thermometer. Add several tofu triangles at a time and fry, turning once, until golden on all sides (4 to 5 minutes). Remove from oil and drain on paper towels. Cool, cover, and chill, if made ahead. Remove oil from wok.

Return wok to high heat. When wok is hot, add 1 tablespoon oil. When oil is hot, add garlic and stir-fry for about 30 seconds. Add lettuce, and stir-fry just until lettuce begins to wilt (about 1 minute). Stir in peas and mushrooms; top with stuffed tofu. Pour broth over tofu, cover, and simmer until tofu is hot (3 to 5 minutes if tofu is warm or at room temperature, 10 to 12 minutes if cold).

Mix together cornstarch, soy sauce, and water. Push tofu away from one side of wok and stir soy mixture into broth. Cook, stirring carefully so as not to break up tofu, until the sauce boils and thickens (about 1 minute). Makes 2 or 3 servings.

Fish stuffing. Finely chop ¼ pound **boneless lean white fish fillets** (such as rockfish or turbot). Mix fish with 2 teaspoons minced **green onion;** ¾ teaspoon **soy sauce;** ¼ teaspoon *each* **cornstarch, salad oil,** and **sesame oil** (optional); ⅛ teaspoon *each* **salt, sugar,** and **liquid hot pepper seasoning;** and dash **pepper.**

Deep-fried Sweet and Sour Pork

Sweet and sour pork is a favorite dish found on many Chinese menus. This recipe combines crisply fried nuggets of pork with green pepper and pineapple in a sweet-sour sauce. Serve it over hot cooked rice.

Seasoning sauce (directions follow)
1 egg yolk
2 teaspoons water
1 tablespoon *each* all-purpose flour
    and cornstarch
1 pound boneless pork, cut into
    1-inch cubes
    Salad oil
1 clove garlic, minced or pressed
2 green peppers, seeded and cut into
    ¼-inch-wide strips
1 can (13 oz.) pineapple tidbits, drained
    Hot cooked rice

Prepare seasoning sauce and set aside.

Beat egg yolk with water; blend in flour and cornstarch until smooth. Add cubes of pork and mix to coat meat well; drain off excess.

Place wok in ring stand. Pour oil into wok to a depth of about 1½ inches and heat to 340° on a deep-fat-frying thermometer. Add meat and fry, stirring occasionally, until golden brown (10 to 12 minutes). Remove with a slotted spoon, drain, and keep warm.

Remove all but 2 tablespoons of the oil from wok. Place wok directly over medium-high heat. When oil is hot, add garlic and stir until lightly browned. Add green pepper and stir-fry for about 1 minute. Add pineapple tidbits, seasoning sauce, and meat; stir until mixture boils and thickens (about 1 minute). Serve over hot cooked rice. Makes 3 servings.

Seasoning sauce. Mix together ¾ cup **water** and 1 tablespoon **cornstarch** until smooth. Stir in 1 tablespoon *each* **catsup** and **soy sauce,** 4 tablespoons *each* **sugar** and **wine vinegar,** and a few drops **liquid hot pepper seasoning.**

Thai Crunchy Noodles

Crunchy Thai rice noodles mix with pork, chicken, and shrimp in a rich sauce. Fresh bean sprouts and green onions dress up the dish. The dried, opaque, white, thin rice noodles (also called rice sticks or mai fun) aren't to be confused with bean threads (sometimes called translucent noodles); (see photograph on page 10). They can be fried a day ahead, stored airtight, then reheated in a 200° oven for 10 minutes.

(Continued on page 63)

*Puffing up when they hit hot oil, bean threads
cook in an instant. Combine with chicken and coriander for
Chinese chicken salad. The recipe is on page 63.*

¼ cup *each* sugar, lime juice, yellow bean
sauce (also called bean sauce or
ground bean sauce) and catsup
2 tablespoons soy sauce
Salad oil
¼ pound rice noodles
4 cloves garlic, minced or pressed
1 small onion, finely chopped
½ pound lean boneless pork, cut into
pieces, 2 inches long and ½ inch wide
1 chicken breast (about 1 lb.), skinned,
boned, and cut into thin strips 2
inches long and ½ inch wide
½ pound medium-size raw shrimp, shelled
and deveined
½ pound bean sprouts
4 green onions, cut into 4-inch pieces
1 lime, cut in wedges

Stir together sugar, lime juice, bean sauce, cat-sup, and soy; set aside.

Place wok in ring stand. Pour oil into wok to a depth of about 1 inch and heat to 375° on a deep-fat-frying thermometer. Drop in a small handful of noodles at a time. As they puff and expand, immediately push them down into oil with 2 spatulas, then turn over entire mass to be sure all are cooked. As soon as noodles stop crackling (about 15 seconds), remove with slotted spoon and drain. As you continue frying, frequently skim off and discard any bits of noodles remaining in oil. Keep noodles warm in a 200° oven until serving time. Remove oil from wok.

Place wok over high heat. When wok is hot, add 2 tablespoons oil. When oil is hot, add garlic and onion; stir-fry for about 1 minute. Add pork and stir-fry for about 3 minutes. Add chicken and shrimp and stir-fry for about 4 minutes or until shrimp turns pink. Add bean sauce mixture, bring to a boil, and cook for 1 minute. Remove from heat and cool for 3 minutes.

Gently fold in fried noodles, a portion at a time, until all are lightly coated with sauce. Mound in center of a large platter and surround with bean sprouts. Garnish with green onion and lime wedges. Makes 4 servings.

Chinese Chicken Salad

Pictured on facing page

Crisp curly strands of translucent Oriental noodles are combined with deep-fried chicken, toasted sesame seed, and pungent coriander (cilantro or Chinese parsley) in a full-meal salad.

Before they are cooked, the noodles look like stiff nylon fishing line, but they puff up crisp when dropped into hot oil. Look for them in the Oriental section of your market. They are sometimes called bean threads or Chinese vermicelli (don't use taro-based shirataki). Both chicken and noodles can be done a day ahead. Wrap the cooked noodles airtight and store at room temperature until used.

¼ cup sesame seed
¼ cup all-purpose flour, unsifted
1 tablespoon cornmeal
½ teaspoon *each* Chinese five-spice or
ground ginger and salt
Dash of pepper
1 broiler-fryer chicken (about 2½ lbs.),
split in half
Salad oil
Seasoning sauce (directions follow)
½ medium-size head iceberg lettuce,
thinly shredded
3 green onions, thinly sliced (optional)
1 small bunch fresh coriander (cilantro
or Chinese parsley)
2 or 3 ounces translucent noodles

Place wok over medium heat. When wok is hot, add sesame seed and stir-fry until golden (about 2 minutes); set aside.

Mix together flour, cornmeal, Chinese five-spice, salt, and pepper. Dredge chicken in mixture to coat all over; shake off excess.

Place wok in ring stand. Pour oil into wok to a depth of about 2 inches and heat to 375° on a deep-fat-frying thermometer. Add chicken halves, turning as needed, until well browned on all sides (about 15 minutes); drain and cool.

Meanwhile, prepare seasoning sauce and set aside.

Skin, bone, and cut cooled chicken and the crispy skin into match-stick-size pieces; place in a large bowl. Add lettuce and onion. Pull off cilantro leaves (you should have 1 to 2 cups) and add to salad. Sprinkle with sesame seed, drizzle with Chinese seasoning sauce, and refrigerate.

Reheat oil in wok to 375°. Drop in handfuls of noodles at a time. As they puff and expand, immediately push them down into oil with 2 spatulas, then turn over entire mass to be sure all are cooked. As soon as noodles stop crackling (about 30 seconds), remove with strainer and drain. As you continue frying, frequently skim off and discard any bits of noodles remaining in oil. Mix noodles into salad thoroughly just before serving on individual plates. Makes 4 servings.

Seasoning sauce. Combine ½ teaspoon **dry mustard**, 1 teaspoon *each* **sugar** and grated **lemon peel**, 2 teaspoons **soy sauce**, 1 tablespoon **lemon juice**, 1 teaspoon **sesame oil** (optional), and 4 to 6 tablespoons **salad oil**. (Add ½ teaspoon ground coriander, if fresh cilantro isn't used in salad.)

STEAMING IN A WOK

Cooking with steam is quick and easy,
the results nutritious and flavorful. In steam cooking,
the flavors of the foods mingle more completely than in
other methods of cooking; very little if any fat is used;
vitamin and mineral loss is minuscule; and you can serve
right from the cooking dish. You can enhance
and accent natural flavors by sprinkling seasonings
over foods being cooked.

How to steam in a wok

You can steam anything in a wok—from seafood to poultry, desserts to breads—and master the technique in no time.

The basic equipment for wok steaming includes a ring stand (unless yours is a flat-bottomed wok), a wok lid, and a rack on which to place food in the wok. Other accessories are available, including bamboo steaming baskets with lids that prevent condensation during steaming—see "The steaming technique" on page 8 and the photograph on page 7.

Place the wok in a ring stand over the burner or element of your range. Add 1½ to 2 inches hot water. Place a metal rack directly over but not touching the water. Cover the wok and bring the water to a boil. When water is boiling, place the food on the rack or on a shallow plate to set on the rack—but be sure you don't cover all the steam holes. Cover wok, maintain heat to keep water boiling, and steam for the time specified in your recipe or in the chart for steaming vegetables (page 66). Otherwise, cook for the same amount of time as you would if you were simmering the food *in* water.

During cooking, some steam will condense and form drops of water under the wok lid. To shield the food from such moisture, some cooks drape a piece of wax paper over it.

Check the water level every once in awhile through cooking to make sure the wok doesn't dry out; add water as needed.

Carefully remove the food from the steaming rack with a large spatula (two if you have them).

Italian Sausage and Grapes with Green Beans

Juicy hot grapes provide a sweet-tart contrast to the lively seasonings of Italian sausage and the mildness of green beans. You may use your wok for each stage of this quickly prepared entrée.

       About 1 pound mild Italian sausage
    1 pound green beans, ends and
          strings removed
       Salt
    2 tablespoons butter or margarine
    1½ cups (½ lb.) Thompson seedless grapes

Place sausage on one side of rack in wok over 1½ to 2 inches boiling water. Cover and steam for 10 minutes. Place beans on other side of rack, sprin-

kle lightly with salt, cover, and continue steaming until beans are tender (about 10 minutes).

Transfer beans to a serving dish and cover to keep warm. Remove sausage from wok and cut in ½-inch-thick slices.

Remove rack from wok, drain water, and return wok to medium-high heat. When wok is hot, add butter. When butter has melted, add sausage and stir-fry until lightly browned (about 3 minutes). Add grapes and stir-fry until grapes are heated through (about 1 minute). Pour meat and fruit over or alongside beans. Makes 4 servings.

Pearl Balls

These savory meatballs wear a spangled coating of glutinous rice which becomes translucent during steaming. Look for the rice, also called sweet rice or mochi rice, in Oriental food stores; you cannot use long grain rice as a substitute.

    ⅔ cup glutinous rice
    4 dried Chinese mushrooms
    1 pound boneless pork butt, finely
          chopped or ground
    4 water chestnuts, finely chopped
    1 green onion, finely chopped
    1 egg
    1 teaspoon *each* salt, cornstarch, dry
          sherry, and finely chopped fresh
          ginger root
    ½ teaspoon sugar
    1 tablespoon soy sauce

Cover rice with cold water and let soak for 2 hours; drain and spread on a plate. Cover mushrooms with hot water and let soak for 30 minutes. Cut off and discard stems; squeeze mushrooms dry and finely chop. Combine mushrooms, pork, water chestnuts, and green onion. Beat egg lightly with salt, cornstarch, sherry, ginger, sugar, and soy. Add to meat mixture and mix lightly.

With wet hands, roll meat mixture, 2 tablespoons at a time, into balls. (Shape smaller, marble-size balls for hors d'oeuvres.) Roll each ball in glutinous rice to coat completely; arrange on a heatproof plate, allowing ½-inch space between balls.

Place plate on rack in wok over 1½ to 2 inches boiling water. Cover wok and steam for 45 minutes (adding more water as it evaporates) or until meat is no longer pink and rice is pearl-like. Makes 4 or 5 servings.

Beef balls with glutinous rice. Follow directions for pearl balls with the following changes: Omit

(Continued on page 68)

Steaming vegetables

As a technique for cooking vegetables, steaming is one of the best. Because you cook vegetables *over* rather than *in* boiling water, you capture all of their natural sweetness. Swirling vapors, rather than water, tenderize the vegetables, so there is a minimal loss of vitamins and minerals. And steaming does not require a watchful eye. Simply place the vegetables on a rack set in a wok over 1½ to 2 inches of boiling water; then cover and steam until tender.

Steamed vegetables have a light flavor. They need little seasoning to emphasize their freshness, but you may want to sprinkle them with salt, pepper, and herbs *before* cooking. If you wish to add butter, soy, or other liquid seasonings, arrange the vegetables in a heatproof dish and place the dish on a rack in the wok. Drape wax paper over the dish to prevent condensation from dripping onto the food during cooking; then cover and steam. You can also serve the vegetables in the cooking dish.

The chart below gives cooking times for 1 pound of vegetables. Start counting the cooking time when the water below the steaming rack is boiling rapidly. For long periods of steaming, replenish water in wok as it evaporates.

When the vegetables are cooked, lift the lid of the wok and allow the steam to disperse for a few seconds before removing the food.

If you plan to serve the vegetables in a cold salad or marinate them for a first course, cool them quickly in cold water, drain, and refrigerate.

Vegetable (1 lb.)	Preparation	Minutes to steam
Artichoke, medium-size	Trim thorny tips and stem ends; steam whole	40 to 45
Asparagus	Peel or remove tough ends; steam whole	6 to 8
Beans, green	Remove ends and strings; steam whole	10
Beets, 2-inch diameter	Steam whole; peel after steaming	45 to 50
Broccoli	Cut flowerets in 3-inch lengths; slash stems	10 to 12
Brussels sprouts	Trim ends; steam whole	8 to 10
Cabbage	Cut in 2-inch wedges	15
Carrots, medium-size	Peel; trim ends; steam whole	25
Cauliflower, medium-size	Trim; steam whole	25 to 30
Corn-on-the-cob	Remove husk and silk Remove silk; leave husk on	10 18 to 20
Parsnips	Peel, trim ends, steam whole	20 to 22
Potatoes, boiling, 2½-inch diameter	Steam whole; peel after steaming	30 to 35
Potatoes, sweet, medium-size	Steam whole; peel after steaming	30
Spinach	Remove tough stems; steam whole leaves	4 to 5
Squash, winter	Cut in half; peel after steaming	40 to 45
Zucchini and summer squash	Trim ends; steam whole	20 to 25

*Crowned with sliced mushrooms, chicken tofu custard
steams tender in a wok. With it, serve green onion sauce,
steamed broccoli, and Chinese sausage. The recipe is on page 73.*

the dried mushrooms and green onion. Substitute 1 pound lean **ground beef** for the pork. Add 1 small **onion,** finely chopped. Steam beef balls for 25 minutes.

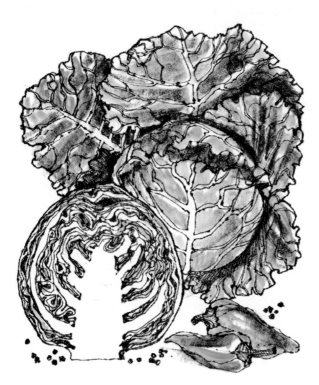

Beef-stuffed Cabbage Leaves

Bright green blanched cabbage leaves, rolled to enclose a filling of rice and beef, steam for about a half-hour in your wok. Accompany with a hot tomato sauce.

    1 large head (about 2 lbs.) cabbage
    2 quarts boiling salted water
    1 pound lean ground beef
    1 medium-size onion, chopped
 1½ cups cooked rice
    4 tablespoons melted butter or margarine
    ½ cup fine dry bread crumbs
    ¾ teaspoon salt
    ¼ teaspoon *each* pepper and rubbed sage
       Tomato sauce (directions follow)

Cut core from cabbage. Holding cabbage under cold running water, carefully remove leaves one at a time, letting water help you separate them without tearing (you will need about 15 leaves). Immerse 4 cabbage leaves at a time into the boiling salted water just until bright green and limp (about 3 minutes). Remove leaves from water with tongs; drain and cool.

Mix together meat, onion, rice, butter, bread crumbs, salt, pepper, and sage.

Place 3 to 4 tablespoons of the meat mixture on largest cabbage leaves (use 2 to 3 tablespoons for smaller leaves) near base of each leaf. With base of leaf toward you, fold leaf up over meat and roll toward tip. Hold roll with seam underneath and fold outer edges of leaf under, making a pillow-shaped roll. Cover and refrigerate until next day, if desired.

In a greased 2-quart round casserole, place cabbage rolls in 2 layers. Place on rack in wok over 1½ to 2 inches boiling water. Cover and steam for 30 minutes (45 minutes if refrigerated). Serve with tomato sauce to pour over. Makes 15 cabbage rolls.

Tomato sauce. Melt 4 tablespoons **butter** or margarine in a small pan. Add ½ teaspoon **salt,** ½ teaspoon **chili powder,** and 2 tablespoons all-purpose **flour.** Stir to a smooth paste. Cook over high heat, stirring, until mixture boils. Remove from heat and gradually stir in 2 cups **tomato juice.** Return to heat and cook until it boils and thickens.

Corned Beef and Frosted Cabbage Wedges

A large piece of corned beef fits nicely under the dome-shaped wok lid. Beer is added to the seasoned steaming bath for an enticing flavor. You may want to reheat any leftover meat in the steamer and use it for sandwiches.

    1 bay leaf
    1 stick cinnamon
    1 small dried hot chile pepper
    ½ teaspoon *each* whole coriander, whole
       allspice, and mustard seed
    1 can (12 oz.) beer
    3 pounds corned beef
    1 medium-size head (about 1½ lbs.)
       cabbage
    ¼ cup *each* mayonnaise and prepared
       mustard
    ½ teaspoon dried basil leaves

Place bay leaf, cinnamon, chile pepper, coriander, allspice, and mustard seed in bottom of wok. Add beer, then pour in enough water to make 2 inches liquid. Place rack in wok over seasoned water; place corned beef on rack. Cover wok and steam until meat is fork tender (about 2 hours), adding water to wok as it evaporates.

Meanwhile, cut cabbage into 8 wedges. Combine

mayonnaise, prepared mustard, and basil; cover and refrigerate.

When corned beef is tender, place cabbage wedges over and around meat. Cover wok and steam until cabbage is tender-crisp (about 15 minutes).

Remove corned beef from wok, cut into slices, and arrange on a serving plate. Transfer cabbage wedges to platter and spoon mayonnaise dressing over top of each wedge. Makes 4 to 6 servings.

Black Bean Spareribs

A good choice to include in a Chinese meal of several courses, these spareribs require no last minute attention. If you wish to cook them ahead, however, and resteam them before serving, they remain moist and tender.

    2 tablespoons fermented black beans,
          rinsed and finely chopped
    2 cloves garlic, minced or pressed
    1 teaspoon chopped fresh ginger root
    1 tablespoon *each* cornstarch, dry sherry,
          and soy sauce
    ½ teaspoon *each* salt and sugar
    1½ pounds spareribs, cut 1½-inches long,
          then cut apart between the bones
    2 tablespoons salad oil
    1 green onion, thinly sliced

Mix together black beans, garlic, ginger, cornstarch, sherry, soy, salt, and sugar. Add meat and turn until well coated; let stand for 15 minutes.

Place wok on high heat. When wok is hot, add oil. When oil is hot, add meat and cook for 2 min-

utes on each side or until browned. Transfer to an 8 or 9-inch round heatproof bowl.

Rinse wok. Place bowl on rack in wok over 1½ to 2 inches boiling water. Cover wok and steam for 1 hour or until meat is tender. Skim fat from sauce just before serving and sprinkle with green onion. Makes 2 or 3 servings when served as a main dish, 4 servings when part of a Chinese meal.

Clams with Garlic Butter

Steam clams in an attractive serving container that can go directly from the steaming rack to the table. One dozen clams make a delicious first course for two, plus a bonus—a cupful of rich broth to sip or to spoon over rice.

    1 dozen small hard-shell clams or mussels
    1 small clove garlic, minced or pressed
    1 tablespoon chopped parsley
    1½ teaspoons lemon juice
    2 tablespoons butter or margarine
    1 cup hot cooked rice (optional)

Scrub clams well with a brush under cold water; place in a wide heatproof serving bowl at least 1 inch deep. Sprinkle garlic, parsley, and lemon juice over clams; dot with butter.

Place bowl on rack in wok over 1½ to 2 inches boiling water. Cover wok and steam for 10 minutes or until clam shells open (discard any unopened clams). Lift bowl from wok, dry base with a towel, and serve.

If you wish to serve rice, spoon it into 2 bowls. Arrange clams in each bowl on top of rice, and ladle broth over all. Makes 2 first-course servings.

*Succulent steamed salmon is cradled on a layer
of cheesecloth for ease in lifting it in and out of the
steaming basket. The recipe is on page 71.*

Butter-steamed Fish

Any number of seasonings can enhance the flavor of steamed fish. First dot the fish with butter, then add one of the seasonings suggested in the recipe.

   1 **pound fish fillets, such as rockfish,
       turbot, sole, or sea bass**
   2 **tablespoons butter or margarine**
  ½ **teaspoon salt**
     Dash white pepper
  ¼ **teaspoon dill weed, paprika,
      or grated lemon peel**

Place fish in a round 1-quart pan. Place on steamer rack in wok over 2 inches boiling water. Dot with butter and sprinkle with salt, pepper, and dill weed. Cover and steam for 10 to 12 minutes or until fish flakes readily when prodded in thickest portion with a fork. Makes 2 or 3 servings.

Chilled Steamed Salmon with Lomi Lomi Relish

Pictured on page 70

In Hawaii, lomi lomi salmon could almost qualify as a national dish. It consists of salted salmon combined with chopped tomatoes and onions. Here we propose steamed salmon or turbot fillets served chilled with a lomi lomi-style vegetable relish to accompany each serving.

     Lomi lomi relish (directions follow)
     **About 2 pounds salmon fillets or
       Greenland turbot fillets
       (thawed, if frozen)**
   1 **or 2 bay leaves**
     Peppercorns
     Lemon slices
     Lettuce
     Lemon wedges

Prepare lomi lomi relish; cover and chill for several hours.

Cradle fish on a double layer of cheesecloth that is slightly bigger than the steamer rack. Place fish on rack in wok over 1½ to 2 inches boiling water. Place bay leaves on fish, scatter peppercorns over fish, and top with several lemon slices. Cover and steam for about 10 minutes or until fish flakes readily when prodded in thickest portion with a fork. Gently pick up fish in cheesecloth and remove fish to a plate; cover and chill.

On individual plates, place serving-size pieces of fish on lettuce leaves. Mound lomi lomi relish to one side of fish, then garnish with lemon wedges. Makes 4 to 6 servings.

Lomi lomi relish. In a bowl, combine 2 medium-size **tomatoes** (chopped), 1 large **green pepper** (seeded and chopped), ½ cup thinly sliced **green onion**, 1 small **onion** (chopped), 2 or 3 tablespoons diced canned **California green chiles**, 2 tablespoons **lemon juice**, and 1 teaspoon **salt.**

Chinese-style Steamed Fish

If you steam the fish in an attractive dish, you can take the entreé from the wok to the table. Fresh ginger root is the major flavoring ingredient.

   1 **pound fish fillets, such as rockfish,
       turbot, sole, or sea bass**
  ½ **teaspoon salt**
   1 **teaspoon grated fresh ginger root**
   1 **green onion**
   1 **tablespoon salad oil**
   2 **teaspoons soy sauce**
   1 **teaspoon dry sherry**
   1 **tablespoon chopped green onion**

Place fish in a round 1-quart pan. Sprinkle with salt and ginger. Lay the whole green onion on top of fish. Place on a rack in wok over 2 inches boiling water. Cover and steam for 10 minutes or until fish flakes readily when prodded in thickest portion with a fork.

Remove pan from wok and pour off any liquid from fish; discard whole green onion.

Combine oil, soy, and sherry. Pour over fish. Garnish with chopped green onion. Makes 2 or 3 servings.

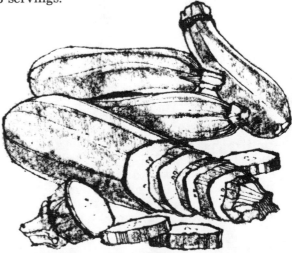

Cracked crab at the beach

Pictured on page 75

When the weather inspires you to a spur-of-the-moment outing, why not pack up your wok and try a beach picnic of succulent Dungeness crab with a savory, spicy broth. You'll need a large (14 to 16-inch) wok for this recipe. You might want to take along the spices from home, but plan to stop en route to buy cooked crabs and any meal accompaniments.

Essential to the enjoyment of this dish is French bread to dunk into the broth. Wrap it in foil and set near the coals to heat. Other accompaniments might include a basket of fresh vegetables, an assortment of fresh fruit, cheese and crackers, dry white wine, and large chocolate chip cookies.

When the time is right, make an open fire or use a portable camp stove. Heat the broth and crab until both are steaming. You can support the wok on several rocks or use the grill of a fire pit, if available.

¼ cup butter or margarine
1 large onion, cut in rings
2 cloves garlic, minced or pressed
½ teaspoon liquid hot pepper seasoning
⅛ teaspoon cayenne
¼ cup chopped parsley
1 bay leaf
2 to 3 cans (14 oz. *each*) regular-strength chicken broth
1 bottle (4/5 qt.) dry white wine
2 to 3 cooked Dungeness crabs (about 2 lbs. *each*), cracked and cleaned
French sourdough bread

Place wok over a hot fire. When wok is hot, add butter, onion, and garlic. Stir until onion is limp (about 2 minutes). Add hot pepper seasoning, cayenne, parsley, bay leaf, 2 cans chicken broth, and wine; heat to simmering. Add crab and simmer for about 10 minutes or until crab is heated through. Add more broth, if needed.

Ladle crab into bowls or deep plates and dunk bread into broth; eat crab with your fingers. Serve broth in cups to drink, if you wish. Serves 4 to 6.

Szechwan Fish Rolls

Mellow-flavored fish rolls make a delicious and unusual first course or light luncheon entrée. The components—wrappers, filling, and sauce—can all be made a day ahead.

Egg wrappers (directions follow)
1 pound boneless sole fillets
1 green onion, finely chopped
1 tablespoon finely chopped fresh ginger root
½ teaspoon salt
⅛ teaspoon white pepper
2 tablespoons salad oil
1 tablespoon *each* sesame oil, dry sherry, and cornstarch
1 egg, separated
Green onion sauce (directions follow)

If made ahead and refrigerated, let egg wrappers reach room temperature (they tear when cold). Cut fish into ¼ by 1-inch pieces; gently combine in a bowl with green onion, ginger, salt, pepper, salad oil, sesame oil, sherry, and cornstarch. Beat egg white and stir into fish mixture. Beat egg yolk lightly and reserve.

To assemble, lay egg wrapper wedges, lighter side up, on a board. Place 1 tablespoon of fish mixture in the center and dot corners with egg yolk. Starting at wide end, roll wrapper one-third of the way; tuck sides in around filling, and continue rolling toward point of wrapper. Repeat until all wrappers are filled. Arrange fish rolls in two lightly greased 9-inch pie pans.

To cook, drape wax paper over tops of rolls. Place 1 pan on rack in wok over 1½ to 2 inches boiling water. Cover wok and steam for 10 minutes. Remove pan from wok, cover with foil, and keep in a warm oven while you steam the second pan of fish rolls. To serve, arrange steamed rolls on a large platter and pour over green onion sauce. Makes 28 rolls, enough to serve 4 as an entrée, or 6 to 8 as a first course.

Egg wrappers. Whirl 7 **eggs**, 1 tablespoon *each* **water** and **salad oil** or sesame oil, ¼ teaspoon **salt,** ⅛ teaspoon **white pepper,** and 1 teaspoon **cornstarch** in a blender until smooth. You should have about 1¾ cups.

Heat a 12-inch frying pan over medium heat; add ½ teaspoon **butter** or margarine, swirling to coat pan bottom. Pour in ¼ cup of egg mixture, tilting pan to coat bottom evenly. Let cook until top is dry but bottom has not quite started to brown (about 20 seconds). Using a spatula, lift wrapper at one edge and roll onto a platter. Repeat, using ½ teaspoon butter and ¼ cup batter for each wrapper; you should have 7 round wrappers. Cut each wrapper in quarters to make 4 wedges each. If made ahead, stack, cover with plastic wrap, and refrigerate.

Green onion sauce. In a small pan, combine 1½ cups **regular-strength chicken broth,** 1½ tablespoons **dry sherry,** 1 tablespoon **salad oil,** 1 teaspoon **sesame oil,** 1 tablespoon **cornstarch** mixed with 1 tablespoon **water,** dash of **white pepper,** and **salt** to taste. Cook, stirring, over high heat until sauce boils and thickens slightly; stir in ½ cup sliced **green onion.**

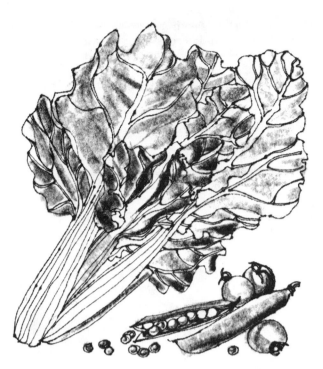

Chicken and Tofu Custard

Pictured on page 67

Chicken and bacon impart the flavor to this low-calorie entrée; tofu adds extra protein and gives it a smooth, creamy texture. Like quiche, this can be eaten hot or at room temperature.

    1 large (¾ to 1 lb.) whole chicken
         breast, boned and skinned
    ¼ pound bacon
    ⅔ cup water
    8 ounces medium-firm tofu (see page 38)
    2 egg whites
 1½ teaspoons cornstarch
    ¾ teaspoon salt
    ¼ teaspoon *each* white pepper and
         sesame oil (optional)
    4 medium size fresh mushrooms, cut in
         ¼-inch-thick slices
    ½ cup regular-strength chicken broth
         Green onion sauce (directions follow)

Use coarsest blade of food chopper to grind chicken and uncooked bacon (or process with a food processor) until coarsely chopped. You should have 1½ cups ground meat.

In a blender or food processor, combine ground meat, water, tofu, egg whites, cornstarch, salt, pepper, and sesame oil; blend until mixture is smooth. Turn into a well-greased 9-inch pie pan, spreading evenly. (At this point you can cover and refrigerate for as long as 8 hours.)

In a small pan over medium heat, simmer mushrooms in chicken broth for 10 minutes; reserve.

To cook custard, place pan on rack in wok over 1½ to 2 inches boiling water. Cover wok and steam for 10 minutes or until a knife inserted in center of custard comes out clean. Remove from wok; tip pan to drain excess drippings. Invert onto a serving plate. Remove mushroom slices from chicken stock and arrange in a band around top of custard; reserve stock for green onion sauce. Pour

sauce over custard and serve in wedges. Makes 4 to 6 servings.

Green onion sauce. In a pan, blend ½ cup **regular-strength chicken broth** (or use the ½ cup reserved broth from preceding recipe), 1 tablespoon **dry sherry,** 1 thinly sliced **green onion** and top, and a dash of **sesame oil** (optional). Blend 1 teaspoon *each* **cornstarch** and **water** and stir into broth. Cook, stirring, over medium-high heat until sauce boils and thickens slightly. Makes ½ cup sauce.

Lemon Chicken

As the chicken steams to tenderness, the marinade changes to a smooth rich sauce, delicious to serve over rice. If you prefer to present the chicken in the traditional Chinese manner, cut the chicken through the bone before marinating in 1½-inch lengths.

    3 pound broiler-fryer chicken
    1 tablespoon *each* soy sauce and
         dry sherry
    2 tablespoons *each* oyster sauce
         and cornstarch
    1 teaspoon sugar
    1 teaspoon sesame oil (optional)
    ½ teaspoon salt
    1 lemon, sliced

(Continued on page 74)

Cut chicken in serving-size pieces; cut breasts and thighs in half crosswise. In an 8 or 9-inch round heatproof bowl, mix together soy, sherry, oyster sauce, cornstarch, sugar, sesame oil, and salt. Add chicken, turning to coat each piece well. Let stand for at least 30 minutes or as long as 4 hours to marinate. Just before cooking, turn chicken in marinade again, then arrange lemon slices over chicken.

Place bowl on rack in wok over 1½ to 2 inches boiling water. Drape a piece of wax paper over bowl. Cover wok and steam for 50 minutes (adding more water as it evaporates) or until chicken is tender. Makes 4 or 5 servings.

Western-style Peking Duck

Pictured on page 78

In this short-cut version of Peking duck, you steam the duck so it sheds much of its fat, then you roast it to brown and crisp the skin. You can serve the Peking duck in the traditional way: Place morsels of the succulent meat on thin rounds of special steamed buns, top with green onion slivers and plum sauce, fold the bun over the filling to be eaten out of hand. You might feature this as part of a Chinese meal or serve it as an hors d'oeuvre.

    1   4 to 5-pound duckling
    ½   teaspoon *each* ground ginger and
            ground cinnamon
    ¼   teaspoon *each* ground nutmeg and
            white pepper
    ⅛   teaspoon ground cloves
    3   tablespoons soy sauce
    5   green onions
    1   tablespoon honey
        Orange slices (optional)
        Fresh parsley or coriander (cilantro
            or Chinese parsley)
        Plum sauce (directions follow) or ½ cup
            canned plum sauce
        Quick thousand-layer buns
            (directions follow)

Rinse duck inside and out and pat dry; cut off tail and discard; reserve giblets for other uses.

Mix together ginger, cinnamon, nutmeg, pepper, and cloves. Sprinkle ½ teaspoon of spice mixture inside duck. Stir 1 tablespoon of the soy into

remaining spice mixture, then rub evenly over exterior of bird. Cut one of the green onions in half and tuck inside cavity of duck. Cover and refrigerate for 2 hours or until next day.

Place duck, breast side up, on a rack in wok over 1½ to 2 inches boiling water. Cover wok and steam for 1 hour, adding more water, if necessary, as it evaporates. Lift duck with 2 large spoons and drain juices and green onion from cavity (save to make soup for another meal).

Set duck on a rack in a baking pan and prick skin all over with a fork. Bake in a 375° oven for 30 minutes. Blend remaining 2 tablespoons soy with honey and brush on duck. Turn oven temperature to 500°. Bake for 5 minutes or until skin becomes richly browned; do not allow skin to char.

Serve whole (garnish with orange slices), or remove breast meat from the bone and cut crosswise in ½-inch-wide strips. Cut legs, thighs, and wings in sections. Arrange meat on a serving plate and garnish with parsley.

Cut remaining green onions and tops in 1½-inch pieces, then cut lengthwise in thin strips. Serve green onions and plum sauce in separate bowls.

To eat, put small pieces of skin and meat on a peeled-off round of a quick thousand-layer bun. Top with a few green onion slivers and a dab of plum sauce, then fold layer of bun around duck and eat with your hands. Makes 4 or 5 servings when served as part of a Chinese meal, 6 servings when served as an hors d'oeuvre.

Plum sauce. Beat ½ cup **plum jelly** lightly with a fork; stir in 1½ teaspoons *each* **sugar** and **vinegar,** and ¼ cup finely chopped **chutney.** Makes ¾ cup sauce.

Quick thousand-layer buns. Open 2 packages (10 biscuits *each*) plain (not butter-flavored) **refrigerator biscuits.** Cut each biscuit in half to make 40 pieces. Roll 30 pieces out individually on a well-floured board to make rounds about 2½ inches in diameter (they immediately shrink back to about 2 inches in diameter, and this is the size you want). Roll remaining 10 pieces into rounds about 3 to 3½ inches in diameter.

Brush tops of small rounds with **salad oil** or sesame oil and stack in threes. Cover each stack with a large round, and gently pull dough down to cover stack, tucking under bottom side. Brush bun tops with salad oil and set each stack separately on a small square of oiled or greased foil. (You can cover buns and chill for several hours.)

Arrange buns, each on its foil square, on rack in wok over 1½ to 2 inches simmering water. Do not put one stack on top of another; cook in sequence, if necessary. Cover wok and steam for 10 to 12 minutes or until buns look rather translucent and no longer feel soft and sticky. Peel apart to eat. Makes 10 buns.

*Tote your wok to the beach to cook fresh crab
in garlicky broth. The recipe is on page 72. Pick up
picnic makings at a market on your way.*

Sweets from the steamer

There's an old-fashioned quality to desserts and breads that are cooked in a steamer. The delicious flavors have never gone out of style, but many cooks overlook this kind of recipe because they lack the equipment or time. With your wok as a steamer, and these updated techniques, you can easily re-create desserts from long ago.

Steamed Carrot Pudding

This pudding emerges warm and spicily fragrant, ready to be enjoyed with a light lemon sauce. It will keep for as long as a week in the refrigerator.

> 1 **cup sugar**
> 1 **cup all-purpose flour, unsifted**
> 1 **teaspoon ground cinnamon**
> ½ **teaspoon** *each* **soda, ground cloves, and ground nutmeg**
> ¾ **teaspoon salt**
> 1 **cup finely chopped suet**
> 1 **cup** *each* **raisins and currants (or 2 cups raisins)**
> 1 **cup** *each* **shredded potato and carrot**
> **Lemon sauce (directions follow)**

In a large bowl, mix together sugar, flour, cinnamon, soda, cloves, nutmeg, and salt. Add suet, raisins, and currants and stir until evenly mixed into flour mixture. Squeeze most of liquid from shredded potato with your hands; add potato and carrot to flour mixture. Stir until well mixed.

Spoon batter into a well-greased 2-quart ring mold and press with spoon into an even layer. Cover mold tightly with foil.

Place mold on rack in wok over 1½ to 2 inches boiling water. Cover wok and steam for 1½ hours or until a wooden pick inserted in center of pudding comes out clean. Add water to wok if necessary as it evaporates. Let pudding cool for 10 minutes, then turn out on rack to cool further. Serve warm with lemon sauce. To reheat, turn pudding back in mold and cover (or wrap slices in foil) and steam again for 30 minutes. Makes 8 servings.

Lemon sauce. In a small pan, combine ½ cup **sugar**, 1 tablespoon **cornstarch**, and dash of **salt**. Stir in 1 cup **water**. Bring to a boil and cook, stirring, until clear and thickened (about 1 minute); remove from heat. Mix 1 **egg yolk** with 3 tablespoons **lemon juice**. Stir sauce slowly into egg-lemon juice mixture. Add 1 tablespoon **butter** or margarine and stir until melted. Serve warm or at room temperature. Makes 1 cup sauce.

Brown Bread

For supper, try thick slices of this dark, moist bread with baked beans and your favorite sausages. Cooked in a ring mold or in small loaf pans, it steams in half the time usually required for brown bread.

> 2 **tablespoons melted butter or margarine**
> ⅓ **cup firmly packed brown sugar**
> 2 **tablespoons light molasses**
> 1 **cup buttermilk**
> 1 **cup whole wheat flour, unsifted**
> ¼ **cup** *each* **all-purpose flour (unsifted) and wheat germ**
> 1 **teaspoon soda**
> ½ **teaspoon salt**
> ½ **cup raisins or currants**

In a large bowl, place butter, brown sugar, and molasses; beat until smooth, then stir in buttermilk. In a separate bowl, stir together whole wheat flour, all-purpose flour, wheat germ, soda, and salt until thoroughly blended. Add to buttermilk mixture and beat until well combined. Stir in raisins. Spoon batter into a well-greased 1½-quart ring mold or two 5 by 3-inch loaf pans. Cover mold tightly with foil.

Place mold on rack in wok over 1½ to 2 inches boiling water. Cover wok and steam for 45 minutes (adding more water, if necessary, as it evaporates) or until a wooden pick inserted in center of bread comes out clean. Let bread cool for 10 minutes, then turn out of mold. Serve warm. To reheat, wrap in foil and steam again for 20 minutes. Makes 1 loaf.

Upside-down Gingerbread Cake

If you've ever been camping and wished for a chunk of freshly made cake, try this moist-textured cake which is easy to steam in a wok over a camp stove. For other ideas on camp cooking with a wok, see page 33.

- 4 tablespoons butter or margarine
- ½ cup firmly packed brown sugar
- 1 can (1 lb.) sliced peaches
- 1 package (14 oz.) gingerbread cake mix
  Whipped cream or reconstituted whipped topping (optional)

Generously grease the sides of an 8-inch square pan. Place butter in pan bottom and set over low heat until melted; remove from heat and sprinkle evenly with brown sugar. Drain peaches well and arrange slices over sugar mixture.

Prepare gingerbread cake mix according to package directions; pour over peaches. Cover pan with a double thickness of foil, forming a dome so cake can rise; pinch foil around sides of pan to secure.

Place pan on rack in wok over 1½ to 2 inches boiling water. Cover wok and steam for 45 minutes or until top feels firm when touched through foil. Invert onto a plate immediately; allow to cool slightly. Serve in squares accompanied by whipped cream, if you wish. Makes about 9 servings.

Steamed Apple Dumplings

Choose a good cooking apple such as Rome Beauty, Pippin, or Golden Delicious for this quick dessert.

- 4 large tart apples, peeled, cored, and sliced (5 to 6 cups)
- 1 tablespoon lemon juice
- ½ teaspoon grated lemon peel
- ⅔ cup sugar
- 1 tablespoon all-purpose flour
- ¼ teaspoon ground cinnamon
- ⅛ teaspoon ground nutmeg
  Dumplings (directions follow)
  Half-and-half (light cream)

Mix apples, lemon juice, lemon peel, sugar, flour, cinnamon, and nutmeg in an 8 or 9-inch round baking dish. Place dish on rack in wok over 1½ to 2 inches boiling water. Cover wok and steam until apples are tender (18 to 20 minutes). Using a large spoon, drop 6 dumplings on top of fruit, making a circle around edge of dish. Cover wok and steam for 15 minutes. Remove from wok and let stand for 5 minutes. Serve warm or cold with cream to pour over. Serves 6.

Dumplings. In a small bowl, stir together 1 cup **biscuit mix,** ¼ cup firmly packed **brown sugar,** ½ teaspoon **ground cinnamon,** and ¼ teaspoon **ground nutmeg.** Combine ⅓ cup **milk** and ½ teaspoon **vanilla;** add to dry mixture, stirring just until blended.

Creamy Cup Custard

Cloudlike custard makes a pleasant finish to any meal. With this steaming technique you cook it in only 10 minutes—one third the time it takes to bake custard.

- 2 cups milk
- ¼ cup sugar
- ⅛ teaspoon salt
- 2 eggs
- ½ teaspoon vanilla
  Ground nutmeg

In a pan, combine milk, sugar, and salt; heat until milk is scalded and sugar is dissolved. Beat eggs slightly; continue beating and slowly pour scalded milk into eggs. Stir in vanilla. Pour mixture into 4 custard cups (6-oz. size); sprinkle lightly with nutmeg.

Place cups on rack in wok over 1½ to 2 inches *simmering* water. (Position first cup in center of rack, rather than on one edge, so rack does not tip.) Drape wax paper over cups. Cover wok and steam for 10 minutes. Remove wok from heat and uncover. Lift wax paper, tipping it slightly so condensed water runs off edge of paper, not onto custard. Custard will appear jiggly, but a knife inserted in the center will come out clean. Place cups on rack to cool for 1 hour, then cover and chill if storing longer. Serves 4.

Soy-marinated duckling first steams in a wok,
then bakes golden brown in your oven. Serve with plum sauce
and steamed buns. The recipes are on page 74.

Index

A Handy Metric Conversion Table

To change	To	Multiply by
ounces (oz.)	grams (g)	28
pounds (lbs.)	kilograms (kg)	0.45
teaspoons	milliliters (ml)	5
tablespoons	milliliters (ml)	15
fluid ounces (oz.)	milliliters (ml)	30
cups	liters (l)	0.24
pints (pt.)	liters (l)	0.47
quarts (qt.)	liters (l)	0.95
gallons (gal.)	liters (l)	3.8
inches	centimeters (cm)	2.5
Fahrenheit temperature (°F)	*Celsius temperature (°C)*	*5/9 after subtracting 32*